Employers are responsible for providing a safe and healthful workplace for their employees. OSHA's role is to assure the safety and health of America's employees by setting and enforcing standards; providing training, outreach and education; establishing partnerships; and encouraging continual improvement in workplace safety and health.

This handbook provides a general overview of a particular topic related to OSHA standards. It does not alter or determine compliance responsibilities in OSHA standards or the *Occupational Safety and Health Act of 1970*. Because interpretations and enforcement policy may change over time, you should consult current OSHA administrative interpretations and decisions by the Occupational Safety and Health Review Commission and the Courts for additional guidance on OSHA compliance requirements.

This publication is in the public domain and may be reproduced, fully or partially, without permission. Source credit is requested but not required.

This information is available to sensory impaired individuals upon request. Voice phone: (202) 693-1999; teletypewriter (TTY) number: (877) 889-5627.

OSHA Guidance Update on Protecting Employees from Avian Flu (Avian Influenza) Viruses

U.S. Department of Labor

Occupational Safety and Health Administration

OSHA 3323-10N
2006

Contents

Purpose

This document is designed to serve two purposes:
(1) to provide guidance on health protection to employers whose employees may be exposed to avian influenza (AI) viruses; and (2) to provide technical information (in appendices) about AI viruses and, in particular, about H5N1, an AI virus currently circulating in Asia, Europe and Africa that rarely causes disease in humans but when it does the case fatality rate is high. This document updates guidance on avian flu issued by OSHA in March 2004.

This guidance is advisory in nature and informational in content. It is not a standard or a regulation, and it neither creates new legal obligations nor alters existing obligations created by OSHA standards or the *Occupational Safety and Health Act* (OSH Act). Pursuant to the OSH Act, employers must comply with hazard-specific safety and health standards as issued and enforced either by OSHA or by an OSHA-approved State Plan. In addition, Section 5(a)(1) of the OSH Act, the General Duty Clause, requires employers to provide their employees with a workplace free from recognized hazards likely to cause death or serious physical harm. Employers can be cited for violating the General Duty Clause if there is a recognized hazard and they do not take reasonable steps to prevent or abate the hazard. However, failure to implement any recommendations in this guidance is not, in itself, a violation of the General Duty Clause. Citations can only be based on standards, regulations, or the General Duty Clause.

Introduction

Numerous stories have aired on radio and television or been published in various news media concerning avian influenza and in particular the H5N1 subtype. Unfortunately there is now much confusion about the different human diseases caused by influenza viruses.

Influenza A viruses can cause three distinct diseases in humans: *avian*, *pandemic* and *seasonal influenza*. *Avian influenza* in humans is rare and the most common route of infection is via direct or indirect contact with secretions (nasal, oral or fecal) from infected poultry. Transmission from human-to-human, if it exists, is extremely rare. However, avian influenza viruses have the potential to mutate or reassort and become pandemic viruses; those that can be readily transmitted between humans and those for which the population has little immunity. If these viruses spread throughout the world, the disease caused by them would be called *pandemic influenza* and the new viruses would be called pandemic influenza viruses. Previous pandemic influenza episodes have occurred in two or three waves of 6-8 week duration and spanned a 12-18 month period. After this period, the population will have built up immunity to the virus, either naturally or through vaccination. If the virus continues to circulate in the population and causes disease, it would become an influenza virus that causes **seasonal influenza** (more popularly called human influenza or the flu).

Influenza A viruses are subdivided into numerous subtypes. The subtypes are differentiated by variations in two viral surface proteins, hemagglutinin (H) and neuraminidase (N). Sixteen different H proteins and nine N proteins have been identified. Subtypes are designated by numbering particular combinations of these proteins (e.g., H5N1). Therefore, there are a total of 144 possible subtypes (16H x 9N) of influenza A viruses and all or most of these have been found in wild waterfowl. Interestingly only three of the 144 subtypes, H1N1, H2N2 and H3N2, have caused *pandemic influenza* in the 20th century. Only strains of H1N1 and

H3N2 are currently circulating and causing *seasonal influenza*. Recently a number of different subtypes of influenza A viruses have emerged as agents of *avian influenza* in humans and these include H5N1, H7N2, H7N3, H7N7 and H9N2.

As of October 2006, H5N1 viruses have killed more than 150 people in ten different countries since the beginning of 2003. On the other hand, the H7N7 virus has been associated with a single human death but numerous cases of conjunctivitis (eye infection) in the Netherlands. The H7N2, H7N3 and H9N2 viruses have caused only mild disease in humans. While the number of human deaths caused by the H5N1 virus is small in comparison to the annual deaths attributed to human seasonal influenza viruses (~36,000/ year in the U.S.), it is of particular concern to the public health community because many scientists believe that this virus may continue to mutate or reassort and a strain may ultimately develop the ability to pass readily between humans. If this happens, the virus that emerges may cause the next major influenza pandemic. *As of October 2006, the highly pathogenic avian influenza (HPAI) H5N1 virus has not been detected in North or South America and it is important to understand that a pandemic influenza virus has not yet emerged and when, and if, it will emerge is impossible to predict.*

This document is for current implementation and provides guidance to employees that are likely to become exposed to avian influenza if it reaches the U.S. or if they travel or work abroad. It focuses on the following groups of employees that are at risk of being exposed to *avian influenza* infections, but the list is not intended to be all-inclusive.

- Poultry employees
- Animal handlers other than poultry employees
- Laboratory employees
- Healthcare workers who treat patients with known or suspected AI viruses
- Food handlers
- Airport personnel exposed to passengers suspected of being AI-infected
- Travelers on temporary work assignment abroad

- U.S. employees stationed abroad
- Other employee groups that may be at risk

There are many other employees that may become at risk if there is a serious avian flu outbreak.

> **Notes:**
>
> As much as possible, each section of this document is designed as a stand-alone reference and, therefore, portions of the document are redundant.
>
> The website URLs cited in this document were effective as of October 2006. Be aware that URLs are often changed. If the website URL does not work, go to the home page of the organization. This can usually be done by deleting all of the URL characters after the first forward slash. For instance, if the site is www.cdc.gov/od/oc/media/pressrel/fs021025.htm, the home page would be located at www.cdc.gov. You may then be able to find the web page of interest by following links on the home page.
>
> The appendices are current as of October 2006. Since information is constantly changing, consult the web sites in Appendix I; many of these are updated regularly.

Guidance for Poultry Employees

At the end of 2004, OSHA worked with NIOSH through a joint agency Issues Exchange Group and developed a Safety and Health Information Bulletin (SHIB 12-13-2004) titled, *Avian Influenza, Protecting Poultry Workers at Risk*. The document details safety measures that should be adopted by poultry employees. (See www.osha.gov/dts/shib/shib121304.html).

In addition, the Centers for Disease Control and Prevention (CDC) has issued interim recommendations in a web document titled *Interim Guidance for Protection of Persons Involved in U.S. Avian Influenza Outbreak Disease Control and Eradication Activities.*[1] The CDC recommendations are based on precautions that are considered best practices for protecting individuals involved in the response to an AI outbreak.

The following guidance information synthesizes the recommendations from both the CDC web document and the OSHA SHIB. **The guidance provided should be implemented in the event of a suspected or confirmed avian flu outbreak at a poultry facility.** Recommendations include the following procedures: basic infection control, personal protective equipment (PPE), antiviral drug use and seasonal flu vaccination, medical monitoring of employees and disinfection of contaminated areas. A safety and medical officer should be identified to ensure compliance with procedures. In addition, the United States Department of Agriculture (USDA) (see: www.aphis.usda.gov/vs/birdbiosecurity/hpai.html) and State biosecurity web sites should be consulted for additional procedures for disease control and eradication.

Employees Potentially at Risk
- Poultry farmers and their employees
- Service technicians of poultry processing facilities
- Caretakers at poultry facilities
- Layer barn employees
- Chick movers at egg production facilities

7

- Employees involved in disease control and eradication activities including:
  - State;
  - Federal;
  - Contract; and
  - Company Employees.
- Live Bird Market Employees
- Bird Fighting Industry Employees

Signs that Poultry May Be Infected with AI

Employers should train employees to be alert to poultry that develop one or more of the following signs.

- Sudden death (no apparent symptoms)
- Lack of energy and appetite
- Lack of coordination
- Purple discoloration of the wattles, combs, and legs
- Soft-shelled or misshapen eggs
- Diarrhea
- Swelling of the head, eyelids, comb, wattles, and hocks
- Nasal discharge
- Decreased egg production
- Coughing, sneezing.

Transmission to Humans

Exposure of the conjunctival membranes of the eyes and/or the oral or nasal mucosa to secretions (oral, nasal or fecal) from AI-infected birds is the predominant route of transmission of these viruses to humans.

In contrast, seasonal human influenza viruses are primarily transmitted from person-to-person via nasal or oral secretions only.

Avoid direct contact with bird secretions and inhalation of dust contaminated with these secretions.

Basic Infection Control Measures

- Educate employees about the importance of strict adherence to hand hygiene, especially after any of the following activities:
  - contact with infected or exposed poultry;
  - contact with surfaces contaminated with bird feces or respiratory secretions; or
  - removing personal protective equipment of any kind (e.g., gloves, goggles, respirator, etc.).

  Good hand hygiene should consist of the following:
  - washing the hands thoroughly with soap and water for 15-20 seconds; or
  - if hand-washing facilities are not readily available, use other standard hand-disinfection procedures as specified by state government, industry, or USDA outbreak-response guidelines.

  Consult CDC's website (*Hand Hygiene Guidelines Fact Sheet* at: www.cdc.gov/od/oc/media/pressrel/fs021025.htm) for specific details about effective hand hygiene practices.
- Ensure that personnel have access to appropriate personal protective equipment (PPE) and instructions and training in PPE use.
- Personnel should not eat, drink, or smoke or use bathroom facilities while engaged in activities where contact with contaminated animals or surfaces are possible. PPE should be properly removed and discarded or disinfected. Hands should then be washed thoroughly before eating, drinking, smoking or bathroom use.

  Important considerations:
  - According to a CDC document, *human influenza viruses* can survive for 2 to 8 hours on surfaces. This statement is based upon a single study conducted in 1982 (Bean et al. 1982. Survival of influenza viruses on environmental surfaces. J. Infect. Dis. 146:47-51) and therefore is referring specifically to survival of influenza viruses on stainless steel surfaces.
  - The length of time that *avian influenza viruses* survive after deposit on surfaces varies with a number of environmental

variables. There is even evidence that different strains of H5N1 vary in their ability to survive when exposed to similar environmental conditions (see Appendix D). There have been no published studies to determine how long the virus may survive on surfaces when expelled from a hospitalized AI-infected person.

Personal Protective Equipment (PPE)

Do not eat, drink, smoke, or use bathroom facilities while engaged in activities where contact with contaminated animals or surfaces are possible. PPE should be properly removed and discarded [see section below titled, "Removal of Personal Protective Equipment (PPE)"] or disinfected. Hands should then be washed thoroughly before eating, drinking, smoking or bathroom use.

- Hand Protection
  - Wear lightweight nitrile or vinyl disposable gloves, or
  - Wear heavy-duty rubber work gloves that can be disinfected.

  Important considerations:
  - Avoid touching the face and mucous membranes, including the eyes, with gloved hands that have been contaminated.
  - Gloves should be changed if torn, punctured, or otherwise damaged.
  - Remove gloves promptly after use.
  - Gloves used should be appropriate for the activities, e.g., for some activities it may be more appropriate to use thick rather than lightweight gloves.
  - Long-term use of gloves can result in dermatitis caused by prolonged exposure to perspiration. This can be alleviated by the use of a thin cotton glove worn inside the external glove.

- Body Protection
  - Wear disposable outer garments or coveralls with an impermeable apron over them, or
  - Wear surgical gowns with long, cuffed sleeves, plus an impermeable apron.
  - Wear disposable head or hair cover to keep hair clean.

Important considerations:

- Because protective clothing can be more insulating than regular work clothing, precautions should be taken to protect employees from the effects of heat stress.

- **Foot Protection**
  - Wear disposable protective shoe covers, or
  - Wear rubber or polyurethane boots that can be cleaned and disinfected.

- **Eye Protection**

  Wear safety goggles to protect the mucous membranes of the eyes.

  ## Important considerations:

  - Properly fitted, indirectly vented safety goggles with a good anti-fog coating may be a good choice for poultry employees who have lower risks of exposure (e.g., those employees not directly involved in culling of poultry). However, such goggles are not airtight, and consequently, they will not prevent exposures to airborne material.

  - Employees who wear prescription lenses should wear eye protection that has the correction built into the safety lenses of the protective eyewear, has lens inserts, or can be fitted over regular street-wear prescription glasses without compromising eye or respiratory protection.

  - Eye protection should be fitted together with a respirator because some goggles can alter the fit of a half-facepiece respirator. To ensure that the eye protection does not interfere with a facepiece seal, it should be worn when half-facepiece respirators are fit tested and when employees conduct seal checks each time they put on the respirator.

- **Respiratory Protection**

  NIOSH-approved disposable particulate respirators (e.g., N95, N99, or N100) are the minimum level of respiratory protection that should be worn.

  ## Important considerations:

  - This level of respiratory protection or higher may already be in use in poultry operations due to other hazards that exist in the environment (e.g., vapors, dusts, etc.).

- For farms using oils as dust suppressants, use R or P series respirators.

- Employees who are unable to wear a disposable particulate respirator because of facial hair or other fit limitations should wear a loose-fitting helmeted or hooded powered air purifying respirator (PAPR) equipped with high-efficiency particulate air [HEPA] filters. A PAPR also provides needed eye and mucous membrane protection.

- For employees with substantial exposure to contaminated materials (e.g., those employees directly involved in mass culling of birds), a PAPR may be a practical alternative in a hot, dirty, and wet environment compared to a disposable particulate respirator.

- Note that the particulate respirators recommended above are not appropriate for protection against decontamination or sanitizing chemicals that may be used in disinfection activities (see below under the section titled: Disinfection of Areas Contaminated by AI-Infected Birds).

- Children should not do any work that requires wearing a respirator.

- OSHA requires that respirators must be used in the context of a complete respiratory protection program (RPP). This includes training, fit testing, and user seal checks to ensure appropriate respirator selection and use. To be effective, tight-fitting respirators must have a proper sealing surface on the wearer's face. The elements of a complete RPP are described in detail in 29 CFR 1910.134 (www.osha.gov/SLTC/etools/respiratory/oshafiles/otherdocs.html).

- For information on respirators, see the following: www.osha.gov/SLTC/etools/respiratory/index.html, and www.cdc.gov/niosh/npptl/topics/respirators.

Removal of Personal Protective Equipment (PPE)

- Employees should always remove protective clothing (except for gloves) first and discard or secure the clothing for disinfection before removing their respirators and goggles.

- Remove and discard disposable gloves.
- Wash hands thoroughly with soap and water.
- Keep hands away from mouth and face until hands are washed thoroughly.
- Remove eye protection and place in a designated receptacle for subsequent cleaning and disinfection.
- Remove particulate disposable respirator and discard.
- Wash hands thoroughly with soap and water a second time immediately after all PPE has been removed.
- Disposable PPE should be treated as contaminated material and properly discarded.
- Non-disposable PPE should be cleaned and disinfected as specified in state government, industry, or USDA outbreak-response guidelines.

Important considerations:

- All PPE should be removed carefully to avoid dispersal of contaminated material.
- Hand hygiene measures should be promptly performed after removal of PPE.
- If soap and water are not available, use an alcohol-based hand gel.

Vaccination with Seasonal Influenza Vaccine

- CDC recommends that unvaccinated employees should receive the current season's influenza vaccine.

Important considerations:

- The current season's vaccine will reduce the possibility of co-infection with both an AI virus and a human influenza virus. Although there is only a small possibility that co-infection would occur, if it were to happen, there is the potential for the reassortment of the genetic material from the two viruses with the consequent development of a new human flu virus (i.e., one that is transmissible between people). This novel virus would have the potential to cause an influenza pandemic.

Administration of Antiviral Drugs

- CDC recommends that employees having direct contact with infected poultry or surfaces contaminated with respiratory secretions or feces from infected birds should receive a prophy-lactic dose of an influenza antiviral drug daily for the entire time they are in direct contact with infected poultry or contaminated surfaces, as well as for one week following their last exposure. Antiviral medications are an important adjunct to vaccination; they are not a substitute for vaccination.

For further information about the use of antiviral drugs for influenza, see the CDC web page titled *Prevention and Control of Influenza - Recommendations of the Advisory Committee on Immunization Practices (ACIP)* (MMWR July 29, 2005, Vol. 54:No. RR-8:1-40) at: www.cdc.gov/mmwr/preview/mmwrhtml/rr5408a1.htm.

Medical Monitoring of Employees

- Employers should instruct employees to be vigilant for the development of AI symptoms. These symptoms have ranged from typical human influenza-like symptoms (fever, cough, sore throat, and muscle aches) to eye infections (conjunctivitis), pneumonia, severe respiratory diseases (such as acute respiratory distress syndrome), and other severe and life-threatening complications.

  ### Important considerations:

  - Human AI infections are manifested in different ways dependent on the health status of the individual before infection and pathogenicity of the AI strain. Although the symptoms are, in general, flu-like, they may vary.
    - Individuals infected with the H7N7 virus that caused the outbreak in the Netherlands in 2003 most frequently had conjunctivitis only (see Appendix B for more specific information).
    - Hospitalized individuals infected with strains of the H5N1 subtype most frequently had fever combined with a cough and also had difficulty breathing and/or diarrhea. Conjunctivitis was rare. See Appendix F for specific details

on some of the common symptoms of patients infected with different strains of H5N1.

- Employees who become ill after possible exposure to the AI virus should do the following:
  - Seek medical care but prior to arrival notify their healthcare provider that they may have been exposed to AI.
  - Notify the occupational health and infection control personnel at their facility.
  - With the exception of visiting a healthcare provider, stay home until 24 hours after resolution of fever, unless:
    - an alternative diagnosis is established that explains the patient's illness; or
    - diagnostic tests are negative for influenza A virus.
  - While at home, ill persons should practice good respiratory and hand hygiene to lower the risk of transmission of the virus to others. For more information, visit the following CDC websites:
    - *Cover Your Cough* (www.cdc.gov/flu/protect/covercough.htm)
    - *Hand Hygiene Guidelines Fact Sheet* (www.cdc.gov/od/oc/media/pressrel/fs021025.htm).

Disinfection of Areas Contaminated by AI-infected Birds

After an AI outbreak, it is important that the contaminated areas be disinfected. Depending on temperature and moisture conditions (see Appendix D for more specific details and survival and inactivation of influenza viruses), AI viruses can survive in the environment for long periods, even weeks. However, AI viruses are generally susceptible to the following chemical and physical methods of inactivation:

- Chemical methods
  - Most detergents
  - Specific disinfectants
- Physical methods
  - Heating (the higher the temperature, the more rapid the inactivation)

• Complete drying.

Disinfection in the field is normally done using a chemical method. Viruses associated with organic material such as dust, dirt, litter, and manure may be less susceptible to disinfection because they may be protected from direct contact with the disinfectant.

Certain EPA-registered disinfectants labeled for use against avian influenza viruses are effective for use on hard, non-porous surfaces listed on the label (see: www.epa.gov/pesticides/factsheets/ avian_flu_products.htm for product listings). The label of an EPA-registered disinfectant describes how to use the product safely and effectively and includes measures that persons applying the products should take to protect themselves. The personal protective equipment (PPE) listed on a disinfectant product label is based on the product's toxicity and potential risks associated with use of the product according to the product label. Wearing less protective PPE than specified on the label is considered misuse of the product and a Federal violation. However, employees may wear more protective PPE than required on the label.

Guidance for Animal Handlers other than Poultry Employees

This guidance is for situations in which highly pathogenic avian influenza (HPAI) H5N1 has been diagnosed or is suspected in poultry or wild birds in your area.

While AI is mostly a concern in domestic poultry stocks, other farmworkers, pet shop owners and their employees, veterinarians and their employees, and zookeepers should be alert to any sick birds that show any of the AI-associated symptoms (see: www.aphis. usda.gov/vs/birdbiosecurity/hpai.html). If such birds are observed, immediately notify Federal or state animal health officials or call **1-866-536-7593 (toll-free)** or your local agricultural control agent. Also note that other animals can be infected with certain AI viruses. In particular, H5N1 has been shown to infect cats, pigs and ferrets. These animals should also be monitored for any unusual flu-like symptoms.

If possible, avoid handling potentially infected animals. Allow the Federal or state officials to handle these animals. However, if you

must handle the animals to isolate them from others or to remove dead animals, use appropriate personal protective equipment (PPE). Refer to **Guidance for Poultry Employees** (pages 7-16) for the appropriate types of PPE to wear and also for good personal hygiene practices. A risk assessment by Federal or state officials should assist an employer in deciding the level of PPE that would be most appropriate in a particular situation.

The Department of Health and Human Services (HHS) website at www.pandemicflu.gov provides a web document titled, *Contact Information for State Departments of Agriculture, Wildlife, and Public Health*, which lists contact information for agriculture, wildlife and public health departments for all U.S. states and territories and can be directly accessed at: www.pandemicflu.gov/state/statecontacts.html.

Guidance for Laboratory Employees

CDC has made the following recommendations for laboratory testing for H5N1 in a website document titled, *Updated Interim Guidance for Laboratory Testing of Persons with Suspected Infection with Avian Influenza A (H5N1) Virus in the United States.*[2] Manipulating highly pathogenic avian influenza (HPAI) viruses in biomedical research laboratories requires caution because some strains may pose increased risk to laboratory employees and have significant agricultural and economic implications. Biosafety Level 3 (BSL 3) and Animal Biosafety Level 3 (ABSL 3) practices, procedures and facilities are recommended along with clothing change and personal showering protocols (referred to as enhanced BSL 3 practices). Loose-housed animals infected with HPAI strains must be contained within BSL 3 (Ag) facilities. Negative pressure, HEPA-filtered respirators or positive air-purifying respirators are recommended for highly pathogenic avian influenza (HPAI) viruses with potential to infect humans. The HPAI viruses are agricultural Select Agents requiring registration of personnel and facilities with the lead agency for the institution (CDC or USDA-APHIS). An APHIS permit is also required. Additional containment require-ments and personnel practices and/or restrictions may be added as conditions of the permit.

Important considerations:

- For more information about BSL levels, consult the CDC publication titled *Biosafety in Microbiological and Biomedical Laboratories* (BMBL 4th edition) available at: www.cdc.gov/od/ohs/biosfty/bmbl4/bmbl4toc.htm. A fifth edition is scheduled for release in late 2006.

- If human specimens being examined for the presence of the AI-virus contain blood or body fluids that contain blood, they must be handled following the Bloodborne Pathogens standard (29 CFR 1910.1030). Complete details of the standard are available at: www.osha.gov/pls/oshaweb/owadisp.show_document?p_table=STANDARDS&p_id=10051

- Polymerase chain reaction (PCR) assays or commercial antigen detection testing can be conducted on clinical specimens from suspect H5N1 cases using standard BSL 2 work practices in a Class II biological safety cabinet. BSL 2 laboratory conditions include BSL 1 procedures plus:
  - Biohazard warning signs;
  - Use of leakproof transport containers; and
  - Use of biosafety cabinets (Class II).
    Note: Commercial antigen testing and RT-PCR are not appropriate substitutes for respiratory specimen virus isolation.

- CDC recommends that virus isolation studies on respiratory specimens from patients suspected of having H5N1 infections should only be conducted under enhanced BSL 3 conditions.

- If a clinical laboratory does not have enhanced BSL 3 facilities, virus isolations should not be ordered for patients suspected of having H5N1 infection.

- FDA regulations apply to devices used to test human specimens for avian influenza. Instructions for use may address other precautions, and use of some avian influenza tests may be subject to additional regulatory requirements. For more information contact the Office of In Vitro Diagnostic Evaluation and Safety at: 240-276-0484.

- Use respiratory protection as determined by risk assessment.

- OSHA requires that respirators must be used in the context of a complete respiratory protection program (RPP). This includes training, fit testing, and user seal checks to ensure appropriate respirator selection and use. To be effective, tight-fitting respirators must have a proper sealing surface on the wearer's face. The elements of a complete RPP are described in detail in 29 CFR 1910.134 (www.osha.gov/SLTC/etools/respiratory /oshafiles/otherdocs. html).
- For information on respirators, see the following:
  - www.osha.gov/SLTC/etools/respiratory/index.html, and
  - www.cdc.gov/niosh/npptl/topics/respirators/.

Medical Monitoring

- Laboratory employees should be instructed to be vigilant for symptoms of AI infection for at least one week after their last exposure to AI-infected materials. Symptoms have ranged from typical human influenza-like symptoms (fever, cough, sore throat, and muscle aches) to eye infections (conjunctivitis), pneumonia, severe respiratory diseases (such as acute respiratory distress syndrome), and other severe and life-threatening complications.

Important considerations:

Human AI infections are manifested in different ways dependent on the health status of the individual before infection and pathogenicity of the AI strain. Although the symptoms are, in general, flu-like, they may vary.

  - Individuals infected with the H7N7 virus that caused the outbreak in the Netherlands in 2003 most frequently had conjunctivitis only (See Appendix B for more specific information).
  - Hospitalized individuals infected with strains of the H5N1 subtype most frequently had fever combined with a cough and also had difficulty breathing and/or diarrhea. Conjunctivitis was rare. See Appendix F for specific details on some of the common symptoms of patients infected with different strains of H5N1.

- Laboratory employees who become ill should do the following:
  - Seek medical care but prior to arrival notify their healthcare provider that they may have been exposed to AI.
  - Notify the occupational health and infection control personnel at their facility.
  - With the exception of visiting a healthcare provider, stay home until 24 hours after resolution of fever, unless:
    - an alternative diagnosis is established that explains the patient's illness; or
    - diagnostic tests are negative for influenza A virus.
  - While at home, ill persons should practice good respiratory and hand hygiene to lower the risk of transmitting virus to others. For more information, visit the following CDC websites:
    - Cover Your Cough (www.cdc.gov/flu/protect/covercough.htm)
    - Hand Hygiene Guidelines Fact Sheet (www.cdc.gov/od/oc/media/pressrel/fs021025.htm).

Guidance for Healthcare Workers Who Treat Patients with Known or Suspected AI

The CDC has issued *Interim Recommendations for Infection Control in Healthcare Facilities Caring for Patients with Known or Suspected Avian Influenza*.[3] This document contains the following recommendations:

- All patients who present to a healthcare setting with fever and respiratory symptoms should be managed according to recommendations for:
  - *Respiratory Hygiene/Cough Etiquette in Healthcare Settings* (see: www.cdc.gov/flu/professionals/infectioncontrol/resphygiene.htm); and
  - questioned regarding their recent travel history.
- Patients with a history of travel within 10 days to a country with AI activity and who are hospitalized with a severe febrile

respiratory illness, or are otherwise under evaluation for AI, should be managed using isolation precautions identical to those recommended for patients with known Severe Acute Respiratory Syndrome (SARS). These include:

Standard Precautions

- **Hand hygiene is absolutely essential.**
  - Before and after all patient contact.
  - As soon as possible after contact with items contaminated or potentially contaminated with respiratory secretions.

Contact Precautions

- Use gloves and gown for all patient contact.
- Use disposable equipment (blood pressure cuffs, thermometers) or equipment that can be disinfected before use with another patient (stethoscopes, etc.).

Droplet Precautions

- Wear goggles or face shields when within 3 feet of the patient.
  Important considerations:
  - Face shields are insufficient protection for airborne hazards or for facial splashes.

Airborne Precautions

- Place the patient in an airborne infection isolation room.
  - Airborne infection isolation rooms should have monitored negative air pressure in relation to the corridor, with 6 to 12 air changes per hour, and
  - should exhaust air directly to the outside or have recirculated air filtered by a high efficiency particulate air (HEPA) filter.
- Keep the doors to the patient room closed; this protects other employees who are nearby.
- If an airborne infection isolation room is unavailable, contact the healthcare facility engineer to assist or use portable HEPA filters (see *Environmental Infection Control Guidelines* at www.cdc.gov/ncidod/hip/enviro/guide.htm) to augment the number of air changes per hour.

- Use a fit tested respirator, at least as protective as a National Institute for Occupational Safety and Health (NIOSH)-approved N-95 filtering facepiece (i.e., disposable) respirator, when entering the room.

  Important considerations:

  - OSHA requires that respirators must be used in the context of a complete respiratory protection program (RPP). This includes training, fit testing, and user seal checks to ensure appropriate respirator selection and use. To be effective, tight-fitting respirators must have a proper sealing surface on the wearer's face. The elements of a complete RPP are described in detail in 29 CFR 1910.134 (www.osha.gov/SLTC/etools/respiratory/oshafiles/otherdocs.html).
  - For information on respirators, see the following:
    - www.osha.gov/SLTC/etools/respiratory/index.html, and
    - www.cdc.gov/niosh/npptl/topics/respirators.

Transmission Prevention Strategies in Healthcare Settings

- Place patients that are AI-infected and those that are suspected of being AI-infected together in the same room if private rooms are not available. This would only be a likely scenario if there were a major avian influenza outbreak in your area.
- If possible, try not to place patients with seasonal influenza and those with AI in the same room. Although the risk is relatively small, the sharing of the same room by such patients would increase the chances of co-infection of patients with the two viruses and this could lead to viral reassortment of genes and the possible emergence of a pandemic virus.
- Minimize transportation of influenza patients outside of room.
- Limit the number of healthcare workers caring for influenza patients.
- Limit the number of visitors to influenza patients.

For additional information regarding these and other healthcare isolation precautions, see the *Guidelines for Isolation Precautions in Hospitals* (www.cdc.gov/ncidod/hip/isolat/isolat.htm). The pre-

cautions for healthcare employees listed above should be continued for 14 days after onset of symptoms or until:

- an alternative diagnosis is established that explains the patient's illness or
- diagnostic test results are negative for influenza A virus.

Patients managed as outpatients or hospitalized patients discharged before 14 days with suspected AI should be isolated in the home setting on the basis of principles outlined for the home isolation of SARS patients (see www.cdc.gov/ncidod/sars/ guidance/i/pdf/i.pdf).

Vaccination of Healthcare Workers against Human Influenza

Healthcare workers involved in the care of patients with documented or suspected AI should be vaccinated with the most recent seasonal human influenza vaccine. In addition to providing protection against the predominant circulating influenza strains, this measure is intended to reduce the likelihood of a healthcare worker being co-infected with both human and AI viruses, where genetic reassortment could take place, leading to the emergence of potential pandemic strains.

Important considerations:

- Influenza vaccination of U.S. healthcare workers remains below 40% despite the vaccine's safety and effectiveness. A recent publication clearly describes the benefits of yearly influenza vaccination of healthcare workers. Yearly influenza vaccination of healthcare workers has been demonstrated to reduce absenteeism, nosocomial influenza transmission, and the associated economic losses and disruption of routine operations.[4]

Surveillance and Monitoring of Healthcare Workers

- Healthcare workers should be instructed to be vigilant for symptoms of AI infection for at least one week after their last exposure to AI-infected patients. Symptoms have ranged from typical human influenza-like symptoms (fever, cough, sore throat, and muscle aches) to eye infections (conjunctivitis), pneumonia, severe respiratory diseases (such as acute

respiratory distress syndrome), and other severe and life-threatening complications.

Important considerations:

Human AI infections are manifested in different ways dependent on the health status of the individual before infection and pathogenicity of the AI strain. Although the symptoms are, in general, flu-like, they may vary.

- Individuals infected with the H7N7 virus that caused the outbreak in the Netherlands in 2003 most frequently had conjunctivitis only. (See Appendix B for more specific information).

- Hospitalized individuals infected with strains of the H5N1 subtype most frequently had fever combined with a cough and also had difficulty breathing and/or diarrhea. Conjunctivitis was rare. See Appendix F for specific details on some of the common symptoms of patients infected with different strains of H5N1.

- Healthcare workers who become ill should do the following:
  - Seek medical care but prior to arrival notify their healthcare provider that they may have been exposed to AI.
  - Notify the occupational health and infection control personnel at their facility.
  - With the exception of visiting a healthcare provider, stay home until 24 hours after resolution of fever, unless:
    - an alternative diagnosis is established that explains the patient's illness; or
    - diagnostic tests are negative for influenza A virus.
  - While at home, ill persons should practice good respiratory and hand hygiene to lower the risk of transmitting the virus to others. For more information, visit the following CDC websites:
    - *Cover Your Cough* (www.cdc.gov/flu/protect/covercough.htm)
    - *Hand Hygiene Guidelines Fact Sheet* (www.cdc.gov/od/oc/media/pressrel/fs021025.htm).

Guidance for Food Handlers

This guidance is for situations in which highly pathogenic avian influenza (HPAI) H5N1 has been diagnosed or is suspected in poultry or wild birds in your area.

Although there is no direct evidence that any human cases of AI have been acquired by eating poultry products, raw poultry should always be handled hygienically because it can be associated with many infections, including salmonella. Therefore, all utensils and surfaces (including hands) that come in contact with raw poultry should be cleaned carefully with water and soap immediately afterwards.

Infected poultry stocks should be destroyed before having any possibility of entering the food chain. Ducks can be asymptomatic (with no symptoms) H5N1 carriers and duck products could be unknowingly contaminated with the virus. In 2001, frozen duck meat imported to South Korea from China was contaminated with HPAI H5N1. Once isolated from the meat, the virus was still infective to mice (mice are used as an animal model for testing pathogenicity of avian influenza viruses).[5] In a more recent study, an HPAI H5N1 strain was also found in duck meat imported into Japan from China.[6] Eggs from infected poultry could also be contaminated with the virus and, therefore, care should be taken in handling shell eggs or raw egg products. Fortunately, influenza viruses are destroyed by adequate heat.

Two groups of employees most at risk in poultry food handling are grocery store employees that process raw chicken (butcher it into parts, package parts, etc.) and cooks at restaurants. Grocery store employees should routinely use good hand hygiene when handling raw poultry or poultry products and observe the additional precautions listed below as important considerations after guidance for cooks.

During preparation of poultry, cooks are reminded to follow proper food preparation and handling practices, including the following:[7]

- Separate raw meat from cooked or ready-to-eat foods. Do not use the same chopping board or the same knife for preparing raw meat and cooked or ready-to-eat foods.

- Do not handle either raw or cooked foods without washing your hands and equipment in between.

- Do not return cooked meat to the same plate or surface that it was on before it was cooked or to any surface contaminated with raw poultry.

- Thoroughly cook all poultry products, including eggs and poultry blood. Egg yolks should not be runny or liquid. Poultry meat and eggs should reach a temperature of 165°F (~74 °C) throughout to ensure the destruction of the virus.

- Do not use raw or soft-boiled eggs in foods that will not be cooked.

- After handling raw poultry or eggs, wash your hands and all surfaces and utensils thoroughly with soap and water or an alcohol-based hand gel (if hands are not visibly soiled).

Important considerations:

- Avoid touching your mouth, nose or eyes while handling raw poultry products; the virus could be transmitted in this manner.

- Avoid generating aerosols when cutting up poultry; the virus could be transmitted in this manner.

For more information on good hand hygiene, consult CDC's website:

- *Hand Hygiene Guidelines Fact Sheet* (www.cdc.gov/od/oc/media/pressrel/fs021025.htm).

Guidance for Airport Personnel Exposed to Passengers Suspected of Being AI-infected

This guidance applies to airport personnel potentially exposed to passengers infected with avian influenza (AI). It is not intended for crewmembers on aircraft in operation. The safety and health of crewmembers on aircraft in operation are the exclusive responsibility of the Federal Aviation Administration (see www.faa.gov).

Unless otherwise stated, the recommendations in this guidance section are based on standard infection control practices, available

information about avian influenza, and those portions of the CDC guidance titled, *Interim Guidance for Airline Flight Crews and Persons Meeting Passengers Arriving from Areas with Avian Influenza*[8] that apply to airport personnel.

General Infection Control Precautions

All employees should always follow basic hygiene practices to prevent becoming ill. Many infectious diseases can be spread by human hands. Soiled hands are an effective means of delivering infectious material (e.g., saliva or other body fluids that may contain viruses) to the nose or eyes, where they can enter the body. Hand washing is an important way to reduce exposure to common infectious diseases. Cleaning one's hands with soap and water removes potentially infectious material from one's skin. Hands should be cleaned before preparing food, eating, or touching one's face, and after handling soiled material (e.g., used tissues, lavatory surfaces), coughing or sneezing, and using the toilet. Waterless alcohol-based hand gels may be used when soap is not available and hands are not visibly soiled.

If employees are ill, the following steps should be taken:

- If they are ill, they should not go to work, or, if they arrive ill, they should be sent home.
- If they become ill on the job, they should do the following:
  - Cover mouths and noses with a tissue or hands when coughing or sneezing.
  - Put used tissue in a wastebasket.
  - Clean hands with soap and water or an alcohol-based hand gel immediately after coughing or sneezing.
  - Avoid close contact with coworkers.
  - Go home as soon as is practicable.

For more information about these issues, visit the following CDC websites:

- Cover Your Cough (www.cdc.gov/flu/protect/cover cough.htm).
- Hand Hygiene Guidelines Fact Sheet (www.cdc.gov/od/oc/media/pressrel/fs021025.htm).

Procedures for Protecting Airport Personnel in Close Proximity to Passengers Suspected of Having an AI-infection

- In some circumstances, employers may need to provide their airport personnel with respirators (at least a NIOSH-approved N95 or more protective) when it is necessary to protect their health (see OSHA's Respiratory Protection standard at 29 CFR 1910.134).

- OSHA's Respiratory Protection standard requires that respirators be used in the context of a complete respiratory protection program (RPP). This includes initial and annual training, fit testing, and user seal checks to ensure appropriate respirator selection and use. To be effective, tight-fitting respirators must have a proper sealing surface on the wearer's face. The elements of a complete RPP are described in detail in 29 CFR 1910.134. (www.osha.gov/SLTC/etools/respiratory/oshafiles/otherdocs.html).

- For additional information on respirators, see the following: www.osha.gov/SLTC/etools/respiratory/index.html, and www.cdc.gov/niosh/npptl/topics/respirators.

- Airport personnel should wear disposable gloves if touching blood or body fluids. However, gloves are not intended to replace proper hand hygiene. Immediately after activities involving contact with body fluids, gloves should be carefully removed and discarded and hands should be cleaned with soap and water or an alcohol-based hand gel (if hands are not visibly soiled). Gloves should not be washed or reused.

Management of Possibly Infected Airport Personnel

- Employers should train airport personnel to be vigilant for AI symptoms. These symptoms have ranged from typical human influenza-like symptoms (fever, cough, sore throat, and muscle aches) to eye infections (conjunctivitis), pneumonia, severe respiratory diseases (such as acute respiratory distress syndrome), and other severe and life-threatening complications.

- Employers should instruct their airport personnel who become ill with AI-like symptoms after possible exposure to an AI-

infected person to immediately seek medical care but, prior to arrival, notify their healthcare provider that they may have been exposed to AI.

For more information about avian influenza, see www.cdc.gov/flu/avian/facts.htm, and www.cdc.gov/flu/avian/index.htm.

Guidance for Travelers on Temporary Work Assignment Abroad

Geographic Applicability of OSHA Requirements: Private sector employers are required to comply with OSHA standards and other requirements with respect to work performed in a workplace within the U.S., defined by section 4(a) of the OSH Act as the states, the District of Columbia, and various listed U.S. territories. Federal agencies are required by Executive Order 12196 to comply with all OSHA standards with respect to working conditions of Federal employees without regard to their location.

CDC has issued the following notice concerning travel to areas known to have current or past H5N1 outbreaks: *Outbreak Notice - Update: Human Infection with Avian Influenza A (H5N1) Virus in Asia.*[9]

From January 2005 through October 2006, the number of countries with outbreaks of H5N1 infection among poultry or wild birds increased more than 3-fold from 15 to the following 54 countries:[10]

East Asia	Europe, Siberia, Central Asia	Africa
Cambodia	Afghanistan	Burkina Faso
China	Albania	Cameroon
India	Austria	Djibouti
Indonesia	Azerbaijan	Egypt
Japan	Bosnia-Herzegovina	Ivory Coast
Lao PDR (Laos)	Bulgaria	Niger
Malaysia	Croatia	Nigeria
Mongolia	Cyprus	Sudan
	Czech Republic	

East Asia	Europe, Siberia, Central Asia	Africa
South Korea (Republic of Korea) Thailand Vietnam	Denmark France Georgia Germany Greece Hungary India Iran Iraq Israel Italy Jordan Kazakhstan Pakistan Poland Romania Russia (Siberia & European Russia) Saudi Arabia Serbia Slovakia Slovenia Spain Sweden Switzerland Turkey Ukraine	

In November of 2005, human cases had been reported from only 5 countries. As of October 12, 2006, the number of countries with human cases had doubled to the following 10 countries: Azerbaijan, Cambodia, China, Djibouti, Egypt, Indonesia, Iraq, Thailand, Turkey and Vietnam. Since this information is constantly changing, consult the U.S. Government pandemic influenza website at: www.pandemicflu.gov/, where regularly updated information on cases in both birds and humans worldwide can be accessed. Appendix I contains websites that provide additional information.

To reduce the risk of infection, CDC recommends that Americans visiting areas where outbreaks of H5N1 infection among poultry or human cases of H5N1 infection have been reported should observe the following measures to help avoid illness.

Before Any International Travel

- Always educate yourself and others who may be traveling with you about any disease risks and other travel conditions in areas you plan to visit (for information about H5N1, see the following CDC web page at: www.cdc.gov/flu/avian/index.htm and State Department Travel Warnings and Consular Information sheets at: www.travel.state.gov/travel/travel_1744.html).

- Be sure that your vaccinations are up-to-date and see your doctor or healthcare provider, ideally 4–6 weeks before travel, to get any additional vaccinations, medications, or information you may need. CDC's health recommendations for international travel to Southeast Asia are provided on CDC's Travelers' Health website: www.cdc.gov/travel/seasia.htm.

- Assemble a travel health kit containing basic first aid and medical supplies. Be sure to include a thermometer and alcohol-based hand rub for hand hygiene. See the following web page for other suggested items: www.cdc.gov/travel/illness_injury_abroad.htm.

- Before you leave, find out how and where to get medical care in the country where you are traveling.

- Check your health insurance plan or get additional insurance that covers medical evacuation in case you become ill. Information about medical evacuation services is provided on the U.S. Department of State web page titled, Medical Information for Americans Traveling Abroad (travel.state.gov/travel/tips/health/health_1185.html).

During Travel

- Avoid all direct contact with poultry, even if they appear healthy and especially if they appear sick or are dead.
- Avoid places where live poultry are raised or kept (e.g., poultry farms and bird markets).
- Avoid handling surfaces contaminated with poultry feces or respiratory secretions. The major source of human infections is associated with contact with these substances.

- As with other infectious illnesses, one of the most important preventive practices is careful and frequent handwashing. Cleaning your hands often, using soap and water (or waterless alcohol-based hand rubs when soap is not available and hands are not visibly soiled), removes potentially infectious material from your skin and helps prevent disease transmission.

- *Handwashing is especially important* when preparing raw poultry for cooking.

- Influenza viruses are destroyed by heat; therefore, as a precaution, all foods from poultry, including eggs and poultry blood, should be thoroughly cooked. See International Food Safety Authorities Network (INFOSAN) for guidelines about food safety and H5N1 at: www.who.int/foodsafety/micro/avian/en/. Also consult the USDA website on safe food handling at: www.fsis.usda.gov/Fact_Sheets/Safe_Food_Handling_Fact _Sheets/.

- If you have a fever and respiratory symptoms (cough or shortness of breath) or if you have any illness that requires prompt medical attention, a U.S. consular officer can assist you in locating medical services and informing your family or friends. See the following web page for more information about what to do if you become ill while abroad: www.cdc.gov/travel/illness_injury_abroad.htm. It is advisable that you defer travel until you are free of symptoms unless your travel is health-related.

    Important considerations:

- It is possible that you might become infected in a country where the healthcare systems may be inadequate to cope with human avian influenza.

- If an avian influenza virus develops the ability to pass freely from human to human while you are in an affected country, it is possible that either U.S. or foreign country borders will be closed and return travel to the U.S. may be impossible or delayed.

After Your Return

- Monitor your health for 10 days.

- If you become ill with fever and develop a cough or difficulty

breathing, or if you develop any illness during this 10-day period, consult a healthcare provider. Before you visit a healthcare setting, tell the provider the following:

- your symptoms;
- where you traveled; and
- if you have had direct poultry contact or contact with a known or suspected human case of influenza A (H5N1) in an H5N1-affected country.

More information about the following subjects can be obtained by visiting the websites listed below:

H5N1 infections in humans

- World Health Organization (WHO) website (www.who.int/topics/avian_influenza/en/), and
- CDC website (www.cdc.gov/flu/avian/index.htm).

Recommendations for enhanced surveillance and infection control precautions for H5N1

- CDC website (www.cdc.gov/flu/avian/professional/han081304.htm).

Health recommendations for travel to Asia

- CDC website (www.cdc.gov/travel/seasia.htm), and
- CDC website (www.cdc.gov/travel/eastasia.htm).

Guidance for U.S. Employees Stationed Abroad

Geographic Applicability of OSHA Requirements: Private sector employers are required to comply with OSHA standards and other requirements with respect to work performed in a workplace within the U.S., defined by section 4(a) of the OSH Act as the states, the District of Columbia, and various listed U.S. territories. Federal agencies are required by Executive Order 12196 to comply with all OSHA standards with respect to working conditions of Federal employees without regard to their location.

CDC has issued recommendations for expatriates and U.S. Embassy officials living in areas with past or present H5N1 outbreaks titled, *Update: Guidelines and Recommendations, Interim Guidance about Avian Influenza A(H5N1) for U.S. Citizens Living Abroad.*[7]

CDC continues to recommend surveillance, diagnostic evaluation, and infection control for suspected H5N1 cases in travelers to the U.S. These recommendations are contained in a health update on February 4, 2005 (www.cdc.gov/flu/avian/professional/han020405.htm).

CDC remains in communication with WHO and continues to closely monitor the H5N1 situation in Asia. Updated information can be found at the following websites:

- CDC's Avian Influenza (Bird Flu) web page (www.cdc.gov/flu/avian/index.htm).
- CDC's Travelers' Health web page (www.cdc.gov/travel).
- WHO website (www.who.int/en).

Precautions

- Avoid all contact with poultry (e.g., chickens, ducks, geese, pigeons, quail) or any wild birds, and avoid areas where H5N1-infected poultry may be present, such as commercial or backyard poultry farms and live poultry markets.
- Do not eat uncooked or undercooked poultry or poultry products, including dishes made with uncooked poultry blood.
- As with other infectious illnesses, one of the most important preventive practices is careful and frequent handwashing. Cleaning your hands often, using soap and water (or waterless, alcohol-based hand rubs when soap is not available and hands are not visibly soiled) removes potentially infectious materials from your skin and helps prevent disease transmission.
- CDC does not recommend the routine use of masks or other personal protective equipment while in public areas.

When Preparing Food

During preparation of poultry, cooks are reminded to follow proper food preparation and handling practices, including:[7]

- Separate raw meat from cooked or ready-to-eat foods. Do not use the same chopping board or the same knife for preparing raw meat and cooked or ready-to-eat foods.

- Do not handle either raw or cooked foods without washing your hands in between.

- Do not return cooked meat to the same plate or surface that it was on before it was cooked or to any surface contaminated with raw poultry.

- Thoroughly cook all poultry products, including eggs and poultry blood. Egg yolks should not be runny or liquid. Poultry meat and eggs should reach a temperature of 165°F (~74°C) throughout to ensure the destruction of the virus.

- Do not use raw or soft-boiled eggs in foods that will not be cooked.

- After handling raw poultry or eggs, wash your hands and all surfaces and utensils thoroughly with soap and water.

Important considerations:

- Avoid touching your mouth, nose or eyes while handling raw poultry products; the virus could be transmitted in this manner.

- Avoid generating aerosols when cutting up poultry; the virus could be transmitted in this manner.

- It is possible that you might become infected in a country where the health care system may be inadequate to cope with human avian influenza.

- If an avian influenza virus develops the ability to pass freely from human to human while you are stationed in an affected country, it is possible that either U.S. or foreign country borders will be closed and return travel to the U.S. may be impossible or delayed.

For more information on good hand hygiene, consult Hand Hygiene Guidelines Fact Sheet (www.cdc.gov/od/oc/media/pressrel/fs021025.htm).

Precautions If You Become Ill

If you believe that you might have been exposed to AI, take the following precautions:

- Monitor your health for 10 days.

- If you become ill with fever and develop a cough or difficulty breathing, or if you develop any illness during this 10-day period, consult a healthcare provider but be sure to inform the provider of the following before you visit a healthcare facility:

  - your symptoms;

  - where you traveled; and

  - if you have had direct poultry contact or contact with a known or suspected human case of influenza A (H5N1) in an H5N1-affected country.

- The U.S. Embassy or Consulate can provide names and addresses of local physicians.

- Do not travel while sick, and limit contact with others as much as possible to help prevent the spread of any infectious illness.

For information about safety and security for Americans living abroad, see www.travel.state.gov.

Guidance for Other Employee Groups that May Be at Risk

The following employee groups may be at risk under certain circumstances, especially if there is a massive outbreak at a specific area of the U.S. or if there are numerous outbreaks throughout the country:

- Border/Customs Officials
- Employees of Retail/Wholesale Facilities
- Fish and Wildlife Personnel
- USDA Inspectors
- FDA Inspectors
- Department of Corrections Personnel

- Live Bird Market Employees
- Bird Fighting Industry Employees
- Animal Control Employees
- Taxidermists
- Employees Handling Poultry Feces (Crop farmers, landfill employees, landscapers)
- Hotel/Motel Industry Employees
- Commercial Hunting Industry Employees
- Wildlife Biologists Studying Wild Birds

Employers should train employees to use good hand hygiene and to be aware of the symptoms of avian influenza in birds and other animals. Although the types of personal protective equipment that would be required by each of these groups of employees may be different from those outlined under **Guidance for Poultry Employees**, these PPE recommendations may serve as a guide for other employees depending on the risk assessment made by their employers of their possible level of exposure. A risk assessment can be made by contacting Federal and State government agencies that will be dealing with these issues. Many of the agencies that will have up-to-date information can be found in Appendix I.

Most Federal Agencies have posted avian influenza guidance for their employees. Also most states have guidance for employees that would be most affected if there was an outbreak of avian influenza near them. Consult state health departments for updates on outbreaks and PPE guidance if and when an outbreak occurs.

Employee Training

All employees with potential occupational exposure, as described in this document, should be trained on the hazards associated with exposure to influenza A (H5N1) and be familiar with the protocols in place in their facility to isolate and report cases or reduce exposures.

Worldwide Occurrence of the H5N1 Virus

The first outbreak of highly pathogenic avian influenza (HPAI) H5N1 virus was reported in Hong Kong in 1997. Hong Kong responded appropriately by killing its entire poultry population of 1.5 million birds in 3 days.[11] From 2000 through 2004, there were an additional 15 HPAI outbreaks in Asian countries and 200 million birds were killed. The scale of the problem is enormous, especially when one considers that in the 40-year period before 2000 there were just 18 HPAI bird flu outbreaks (none due to H5N1) and only 23 million birds were destroyed.[12] The H5N1 virus was largely confined to several countries throughout Asia until 2005. Among these were Cambodia, China, Hong Kong, Indonesia, Japan, Lao PDR (Laos), Malaysia, South Korea (Republic of Korea), Thailand, and Vietnam. In 2005, different strains of the virus moved north and westward, first to Russia, Kazakhstan, and Mongolia in July and to Romania, Turkey and Croatia in October.[13]

Human cases of H5N1 influenza were first reported in Hong Kong in 1997 with 6 of 18 human infections resulting in death.[14] From December 2003 to November 2005, there have been 126 confirmed human infections resulting in 64 deaths. This is a case fatality rate of approximately 51%. While no new cases were reported from Hong Kong during this time period, cases were reported from Cambodia, Indonesia, Thailand, and Vietnam, increasing the number of countries affected with human H5N1 infections to five. Vietnam had the highest incidence with 92 reported human cases and 42 deaths.[15] The case fatality rate in humans may be somewhat inflated because it appears that many exposed individuals may have had very mild symptoms or may even have been asymptomatic and, therefore, have not been counted in epidemiologic surveys.[16] Although there have been reports that the virus may have been transmitted from human-to-human, this mode of transmission has not been conclusively determined and, if it does occur, it currently seems to be very inefficient.[17] Beyond infecting humans, the H5N1 virus has been found to infect and kill other mammals. It can be transmitted from birds to both wild and domestic felids (cats) that eat infected poultry. However, transmis-

sion from birds to pigs does not appear to readily occur, although there is increasing evidence that it is beginning to occur. Pig-to-pig transmission has not been documented experimentally, but felid-to-felid transmission does occur.[18, 19, 20]

As of October 2006, highly pathogenic avian influenza HPAI H5N1 viruses have not been reported from North or South America. However, in 2004, an HPAI H5N2 strain was reported in Texas and resulted in the culling of chicken stocks in January and August of that year.[21] During the period from 2004-2005, there have been low pathogenic avian influenza (LPAI) H5N2 outbreaks in Italy, Japan, Mexico, the Republic of Korea, and The Taiwan Province of China and the list of host domestic poultry has been expanded from chickens to include ducks, turkeys, and pheasants.[21] The H5N2 subtype has apparently been causing outbreaks in poultry for quite some time and can readily undergo genetic change from low to high pathogenicity. During a 1983-1984 epidemic in the U.S., an LPAI H5N2 virus mutated into an HPAI H5N2 virus within 6 months and resulted in poultry mortality near 90%. Seventeen million birds had to be destroyed to control the outbreak.[14] Similarly, an epidemic caused by a LPAI H5N2 strain in Mexico in 1992 underwent genetic change and converted from an LPAI H5N2 virus to a HPAI H5N2 virus that was not brought under control until 1995.[14] Although the H5N2 subtype has now been isolated throughout the world, with some strains being highly pathogenic to domestic birds, there have not been any reported cases of human infection.

Wild waterfowl are the natural hosts for influenza A viruses and when they migrate they can enhance the spread of a particular viral subtype worldwide.[22] It appears that at least some of the spread of HPAI H5N1 is also occurring via wild bird migrations. From its origin in Hong Kong in 1997, it has moved northward to Lake Qinghai in China, a breeding center for migrant birds that congregate from Southeast Asia, Siberia, Australia, and New Zealand.[23] The H5N1 strains that are migrating westward are genetically almost identical to those that killed wild birds in Lake Qinghai but distinct from those that have caused death in humans in Southeast Asia. It is currently believed that the East Asia/Australian flyway (Pacific Flyway) of migratory birds may carry HPAI H5N1 to the U.S. via Alaska. The University of Alaska and the USDA have been alert to this possibility

for some time. From 1998-2004, over 12,000 samples from wild birds in Alaska were evaluated for influenza viruses but H5N1 was not detected.[24] In addition, since 2000 the USDA has tested approximately 4000 migratory birds in the Atlantic flyway and H5N1 was not detected. Since the summer of 2005, the Department of the Interior (DOI) has been working with the State of Alaska to strategically sample migratory birds in the Pacific Flyway. As of March 20, 2006, DOI has carried out more than 1700 tests on samples from more than 1100 migratory birds. Although twenty-two HPAI isolates were identified, the HPAI H5N1 was not found.

The USDA, DOI and HHS have developed an Interagency Readiness Plan to monitor wild birds for the early detection of H5N1 and other HPAI viruses in the United States. The plan is part of the President's National Strategy for Pandemic Influenza Preparedness and outlines a prioritized wild bird sampling system with emphasis on Alaska, followed by other areas in the Pacific Flyway and the Pacific islands, and finally the Central, Mississippi and Atlantic Flyways. Emphasis is being placed on Alaska since it is at the crossroads of bird migration flyways and scientists believe that if the strains of H5N1 currently affecting Southeast Asia were to spread to North America via migratory birds they would likely arise first in Alaska. In 2006, USDA and its cooperators plan to collect between 75,000 and 100,000 samples from live and dead wild birds as well as 50,000 samples of water or feces from high-risk waterfowl habitats across the United States.[25]

In addition to spreading via migratory birds, the H5N1 virus may also have been spreading through the legal and illegal movement of infected birds and contaminated avian-origin products. The migration of the virus is a matter of great concern, and the sheer numbers of people, pigs, and poultry in Asia also offers a significant opportunity for the H5N1 virus to undergo genetic reassortment (i.e., when two different viruses infect the same bird, the resulting viruses can reassort their genetic material into unique combinations) to a form that can be efficiently transmitted between humans. Since the last pandemic (the Hong Kong flu) in 1968, the populations of human, pigs and poultry in China alone have increased 2-, 100- and 1,000-fold respectively.[26]

Appendix B
Background on the Biology of Influenza Viruses

The influenza viruses are 80-120 nanometers in diameter but they can be ovoid (egg-shaped) to even filamentous (thread-like).[10] There are three major types of the influenza virus: A, B, and C. Although there are many subtypes of the A virus, there is only one known subtype of the B and C viruses. Within each subtype there are many different strains. The subtypes of the A viruses differ in the combinations of the 16 distinct hemagglutinin (H1-H16) and 9 distinct neuraminidase (N1-N9) viral surface proteins.[10] These are the primary antigens of the influenza viruses against which the human immune system develops antibodies; the H antigen is significantly more immunogenic than the N antigen. There are two major ways in which influenza A viruses can change antigenically: via antigenic drift or shift. During **antigenic drift**, a variety of mutations including substitutions, deletions, and insertions produce genetic variation in the surface proteins. A second type of variation, **antigenic shift**, describes a major antigenic change whereby a virus with a new H (with or without a new N) is introduced into the human population.[27] Type A viruses undergo both antigenic shift and drift, while Type B viruses undergo antigenic drift only, and type C viruses are relatively stable. Influenza A viruses cause disease in birds, cats, dogs, ferrets, horses, humans, swine and marine mammals (seals and whales), while type B viruses cause disease in humans and rarely, in seals, and type C occasionally causes a mild disease in humans and swine.[28, 29]

All subtypes of influenza type A viruses can be found in waterfowl (e.g., ducks, geese, etc.), where they normally reside in the intestinal tract and cause little, if any, disease. At times, some of these viruses mutate or reassort (i.e., when two different viruses co-infect a bird, their genetic components can recombine to form a new subtype or strain) and cause disease in poultry (e.g., chickens, turkeys, etc.) that is very contagious and sometimes deadly. This poultry disease is called avian influenza (AI) or more commonly "bird" or "avian flu." When an AI virus causes high mortality in

poultry, it is referred to as highly pathogenic avian influenza (HPAI) virus. In the past, the disease caused by HPAI viruses was more commonly called fowl plague. If an AI virus produces mild infection in poultry with little mortality, it is referred to as a low pathogenic avian influenza (LPAI) virus. It should be noted that the mutation from LPAI viruses to HPAI viruses has resulted in bird flu epidemics in poultry 19 times since 1959.[30]

The genetic material of influenza A viruses is ribonucleic acid (RNA) and it is arranged in eight separate strands. The two genes coding for the viral surface proteins as well as the other genes coding for internal viral proteins can reassort (recombine with other genes) when a host is infected with more than one viral subtype. This can lead to the generation of novel (new) viral subtypes as well as other genetic changes that affect pathogenic-ity. The H5N1 virus is an example where reassortment of genes from three different virus subtypes led to its development in Hong Kong in 1997. Apparently, the H5 gene of a H5N1 strain present in geese in 1996 was retained but its remaining genes, including the gene coding for the N1 surface protein, were obtained from a H6N1 strain from a green-winged teal and an H9N2 strain from a quail.[31]

Although AI viruses do not typically infect humans, confirmed instances of AI viruses other than H5N1 infecting humans have been documented since 2002 and include:[32]

H7 Subtypes

- H7N2, Virginia, 2002: Serologic evidence of infection in one person.
- H7N2, New York, 2003: An infected patient presented with respiratory symptoms and recovered. The source of the infection was unknown.
- H7N3, Canada, 2004: Infected poultry workers developed eye infections.
- H7N7, Netherlands, 2003: Eighty-nine (89) people, mostly poultry workers, were infected. Seventy-eight (78) patients developed conjunctivitis (eye infections) only; five patients

developed conjunctivitis along with influenza-like illnesses (ILIs) with cough, fever, and muscle aches; two patients presented with ILI only; and 4 patients had "other" symptoms. There was a single death of an individual that presented with acute respiratory distress syndrome. Three possible instances of transmission from poultry employees to family members were reported.

H9 Subtypes

- H9N2, Hong Kong, 2003: An infected child was hospitalized, but recovered.

As of October 2006

- HPAI H9 strains have not been reported.
- Only certain HPAI strains of H7N7 and H5N1 have killed humans; almost all human deaths have been caused by the latter subtype.

Appendix C

Genetic Variations in H5N1 Strains and Implications for Human Health

Since the emergence of highly pathogenic avian influenza (HPAI) H5N1 in 1997 [genotype H5N1/97; different genotypes (clusters of genetically related strains) had not yet been recognized], the parent Gs/Gd genotype of H5N1/97 has undergone additional reassortments with unknown AI viruses. The H5N1/97 genotype did not reappear after the 1997 outbreak. By 2001, six new genotypes (A, B, C, D, E and X0) had emerged. From 2002 onwards, an additional eight genotypes (V, W, X1, X2, X3, Y, Z and Z+) were discovered but the Gs/Gd, A, C, D and E genotypes apparently disappeared.[33] The strain that caused the 2003 outbreak in Hong Kong that resulted in two human cases, one of whom died, belonged to the Z+ genotype.[34] The very similar Z genotype is now dominant in Southeast Asia and was responsible for the poultry and human outbreaks in Indonesia, Thailand and Vietnam in late 2003 and early 2004.[33] The viruses that caused poultry outbreaks in South Korea in 2003 and in Japan in 2003-2004 were members of the V genotype; a genotype that has not been associated with human disease.[35,36] It also appears that the H5N1 viruses from the 2004 Vietnam outbreaks are environmentally more stable than those from the Hong Kong 1997 outbreak; the former survived at 37°C for 6 days, compared with 2 days for latter at 35°C.[37]

HPAI H5N1 has been moving northward. A new H5N1 genotype emerged at Lake Qinghai in northern China in May of 2005 and eventually killed more than 6,000 migratory waterfowl.[38] While it is unusual for an AI virus to kill waterfowl, this is not unprecedented for the H5 subtype. A H5N3 strain killed 1,300 terns (wild waterfowl) in South Africa in 1961.[39] It is important to note that the H5N1 genotype that affected wild waterfowl in northern China appears to be a new reassortant virus, combining genetic material from at least two other HPAI H5N1 strains.[38] These do not belong to the Z genotype that affected Southeast Asia. Also it is now known that the strains affecting humans in Indonesia are of a different sub-

lineage of the Z genotype than those that affected humans in Thailand and Vietnam in 2004 and 2005.[40] As of May 29, 2006, there have been no reported human cases of H5N1 in Thailand or Vietnam in 2006 but the number of cases of human infection in Indonesia is greater than for all of 2005 (25 versus 17 total cases in 2005). The Indonesian sub-lineage is particularly virulent since 25 of the 31 persons infected in 2006 have died (a case fatality rate of approximately 80%).[15]

While all of these various genetic variants of H5N1 are still classified as HPAI strains, some appear to be non-infectious while others are infectious to humans. The strains of H5N1 migrating north and west from Lake Qinghai in China have attacked poultry and wild waterfowl in many countries but have caused human disease only in Azerbaijan, Djibouti, Iraq, Turkey, and Egypt as of October 12, 2006. Of the 54 countries with H5N1 outbreaks in poultry or wild birds, human disease has been documented in only 10 of them.

www.osha.gov

Appendix D

Survival and Inactivation of Influenza A Viruses, Including H5N1

Environmental Survival

Survival of influenza A viruses outside of the host varies with the virus subtype, the strain, the host bird from which it was obtained, pH, salinity, temperature and the type of medium in which the virus is suspended. After excretion by water birds, strains of avian influenza viruses (AIV) of five different subtypes (H3N8, H4N6, H6N2, H10N7, and H12N5) remained infective when suspended in lake water for 30-102 days at 28°C and for 126-207 days at 17°C.[41] In the same study it was estimated that the strain of subtype H10N7, the only strain stored at 4°C, would remain infective for 1333 days. Survival of a strain of the H7N2 subtype was variable in different types of chicken manure and ranged from more than 2 days to 6 days at 15-20°C, from 24 – 36 hours at 30-37°C and from 15 to 20 minutes at 56°C.[42] Another study using a strain from each of three different AIV subtypes (H4N6, H6N2, and H10N7) found that pH, temperature and salinity affected survival of these viruses differently.[43] It can be seen from these studies that many variables affect the environmental survival of AIVs. Therefore, one can only conclude with confidence that AIV viruses survive less well at higher temperatures and lower pH levels.

There have been very few studies on the environmental survival of strains of H5N1. Although the studies cited below were not totally comparable, these data suggest that like the genetic data, strains which caused disease in Southeast Asia in 2004-2005 are different from the one that caused disease in 1997. Although it appears that environmental survival of H5N1 appears to be somewhat strain-specific, this must be more fully studied.

1997 Hong Kong H5N1 Strains

This strain does not survive complete **drying** at room temperature. Not surprisingly, the temperature at which it is stored affects its survival when in moist feces.

- At 4°C (39°F) it survives for over 40 days without detectable loss in viability.
- At 25°C (77°F) it is inactivated after 8 days.
- At 35°C (95°F) it is inactivated after 2 days.[19]

2004 Vietnam H5N1 Strains

Interestingly, H5N1 strains from 2004 Vietnam outbreaks are environmentally more stable than those from the 1997 Hong Kong outbreak; the former survived at 37°C for 6 days, compared with 2 days for the latter at 35°C.[37]

Inactivation

The following provides a list of physical and chemical methods that are considered effective in the inactivation of influenza A viruses in general.[44]

Physical Methods

- Temperatures of 56°C (133°F) for 3 hours.
- Temperatures of 60°C (140°F) for 30 minutes.
- Acidic pH conditions.
- Complete drying.

Chemical Methods

- Exposure to oxidizing agents:
  - Sodium dodecyl sulphate.
  - Lipid solvents (e.g., detergents).
  - Exposure to β-propiolactone.
- Exposure to disinfectants: bleach, chlorhexidine, ethanol, formalin, iodine compounds, phenolics, and quaternary ammonium compounds.

  ### Important considerations:

  - Chemical inactivation is only effective after physical removal of bulk contamination.
  - The hazards associated with chemical decontaminants can be avoided if instructions for their use are followed closely and appropriate PPE is worn.
  - Use only disinfectants registered by EPA specifically for inactivating influenza A viruses and follow all label safety and use directions (see: www.epa.gov/pesticides/factsheets/avian_flu_products.htm).

Apart from the methods listed above, there are many other methods that can effectively kill these viruses. However, one should use the safest method possible when disinfecting areas known or suspected to be contaminated with the virus.

Appendix E

Transmission of the H5N1 Virus

The information in this appendix has largely been condensed from reference 45 (see Appendix J at pg. 64).

Animals to Animals (Poultry to Poultry)

Infected birds shed virus in respiratory secretions via the oral or nasal routes and in feces. Fecal-to-oral transmission is the most common mode of spread between birds.

- The movement of the virus between stocks occur mainly via the following modes:
  - Contaminated equipment;
  - Egg flats;
  - Feed trucks; and
  - Service crew.

  Important considerations:
  - There is documented evidence that cats can become infected with some strains of H5N1 and that the virus can be spread between cats.
  - It is also possible that cats, dogs, rodents, and other mammals may be able to spread AI viruses by contacting contaminated material with their bodies and thereby transporting it to other poultry stocks.

Contaminated Environment to Humans

Several of the many possible modes of transmission are:

- Self-inoculation of intranasal and conjunctival membranes with contaminated hands.
- Exposure during the application of untreated poultry feces as fertilizer.
- Exposure to contaminated water.
  - Ingestion during swimming or drinking.
  - Direct contact of intranasal or conjunctival (eyelid) membranes.

While the modes of transmission from animal-to-animal and environment-to-human may be similar for most strains of influenza virus, there are notable differences in the mode of transmission from animal-to-human and human-to-human between the 1997 Hong Kong strains and the 2003-2004 Southeast Asian strains of H5N1.

Animals to Humans

H5N1 1997 Hong Kong Strains

Most infected patients were exposed to:

- live poultry within a week before the onset of illness.

For this particular outbreak, there was no significant risk related to:

- eating or preparing poultry products.
- exposure to persons with H5N1 disease.
- exposure to ill poultry and butchering of birds. However, this activity was associated with seropositivity (i.e., serum of individuals contained antibodies to the H5 protein) but no signs of disease.

H5N1 2003-2005 Southeast Asian Strains

Most infected patients had engaged in one or more of the following activities:

- direct contact with diseased poultry;
- plucking and preparing diseased birds for cooking;
- handling fighting male chickens (cocks), in particular making oral contact with the head or beak of the bird;
- playing with poultry, particularly asymptomatic ducks; and
- consumption of duck's blood or possibly undercooked poultry.

Important considerations:

- Although foodborne transmission has been implicated as a route of exposure in a very limited number of cases, it is equally possible that these particular AI-infected individuals may have been exposed to other sources of the virus before consumption of food containing uncooked blood.

Humans to Humans

H5N1 1997 Hong Kong Strains

- Did not occur through general social contact, and serologic studies of exposed healthcare workers indicated that the rate of transmission was calculated to be 4% (seroconversion was observed in 25% of these; most were asymptomatic).
- Appeared to occur in several household clusters and in one case of apparent child-to-mother transmission. Close personal contact without the use of precautions was implicated.
- Transmission by small-particle aerosols was not identified.

H5N1 2003-2005 Southeast Asian Strains

- Serologic surveys in Vietnam and Thailand have not found evidence of asymptomatic infections among contacts.
- In northern Vietnam, surveillance of contacts of patients using modern molecular assays led to the detection of mild cases and an increased number and duration of clusters in families. Although these findings suggest that H5N1 strains may be adapting to humans in localized environments, more confirmatory studies are needed.
- Two studies in Vietnam suggest that H5N1 does not pass from patients to healthcare workers even when infection control measures were not adequate. However, there is one case of severe illness in a nurse exposed to an infected patient in Vietnam.

H5N1 versus Human Influenza

In contrast to strains of H5N1 which are still largely AI viruses with ineffective transmission between humans, the human flu viruses can be readily passed from human-to-human via one of the following routes.

- Inhalation of infectious droplets and droplet nuclei.
- Direct contact.
- Transmission may also occur via contact with contaminated surfaces and subsequent self-inoculation of the nasal or conjunctival (eyelid) mucosa.

Appendix F

Symptoms and Outcomes of H5N1 Infection in Hospitalized Patients

The data in this appendix have largely been condensed from reference 45 (see Appendix J). The type and severity of symptoms and patient outcomes can vary depending on the properties of a particular viral strain and the patient's age and medical status at the time of infection. The following information is based on a number of studies of H5N1 infected hospitalized individuals and only lists the most common symptoms (those expressed in at least 50% of the patients) and lists these in order of frequency. The number of patients studied that were infected with the 1997 strain was 18 while the number infected with 2004/2005 strains was 41.

Symptoms

H5N1 - 1997 Hong Kong Strain

- Fever;
- Cough;
- Rhinorrhea (runny nose).

H5N1 - 2004/2005 Southeast Asian Strains

- Fever;
- Cough;
- Dyspnea (shortness of breath);
- Rhinorrhea;
- Diarrhea.

The most striking difference in symptoms between those infected with the 1997 strain and the strains circulating in 2004-2005, was the high prevalence of dyspnea (shortness of breath) and diarrhea in the later patients. Dyspnea was present in only 6% and diarrhea in 17% of patients infected with the 1997 strain.

Outcomes

H5N1 – 1997 Hong Kong Strain

- Time from onset of illness to death: median 23 days (range 8-29);
- Respiratory failure: 44%;
- Death: 33%;
- Age: median 9.5;
- Age range: 1-60.

H5N1 – 2004/2005 Southeast Asian Strains

- Time from onset of illness to death – median 8-12.8 days (range 4-30);
- Respiratory failure: 80%;
- Death: 78%;
- Age: median was as low as 13.7 in one study and as high as 22 in another;
- Age range: 2-58.

These data indicate that the 2004/2005 strains were more virulent than the 1997 strain. The time from onset of illness to death was shorter, while respiratory failure and death rate were higher in patients infected with the former strains. Interestingly, the death rate was higher in the victims infected with the 2004/2005 strains even though 68% had received some form of oseltamivir treatment. However, it should be noted that oseltamivir treatment is most effective when given as soon as possible after onset of symptoms.

It should also be noted that on rare occasions H5N1-infected patients in Southeast Asia have presented with fever and diarrhea only[46] or severe diarrhea followed by seizure, coma and death.[47] Respiratory symptoms were not evident in these cases.

Appendix G

Importation Ban on Birds from Countries Affected by the H5N1 Virus

According to the U.S. Fish and Wildlife Service, before 2004 the United States annually imported an estimated 20,000 birds from countries before they were affected with avian H5N1 influenza outbreaks. On February 4, 2004, both the CDC and USDA issued orders banning the importation of all birds whether dead or alive, and all bird products, such as eggs, originating from the Asian countries in which H5N1 AI had been documented.[48] These countries have a single asterisk in the table below. Although the CDC and USDA had bird import restrictions for nine countries in early 2004, in just over 2 years the list has almost quadrupled to 36 as of October 2006. The table below lists the affected countries. This information is constantly changing and is updated as H5N1 outbreaks in poultry occur in different countries. The updated lists can be accessed at: www.cdc.gov/flu/avian/outbreaks/embargo.htm and www.aphis.usda.gov/vs/ncie/country. html#HPAI.

Countries Affected by Current (as of October 2006) CDC and USDA Bird Import Restrictions

East Asia and the Pacific	South Asia	Europe & Eurasia	Africa	Near East
Burma (Myanmar)	Afghanistan	Albania	Burkina Faso	Gaza and West Bank***
Cambodia*	India	Azerbaijan	Cameroon	Israel
China*	Kazakhstan	Denmark**	Djibouti	Jordan
Indonesia*	Pakistan	France**	Egypt	
Japan*		Germany**	Ivory Coast	
Laos*		Hungary**	Niger	
Malaysia*		Romania	Nigeria	
South Korea*		Russia	Sudan	
Thailand*		Sweden**		
Vietnam*		Turkey		
		Ukraine		

*The first countries to be placed on the list as of February 4, 2004.

**USDA has specified defined areas of these countries from which bird imports are restricted.

***Palestinian Autonomous Territories

USDA maintains trade restrictions on the importation of poultry and poultry products from countries where HPAI H5N1 has been detected in commercial or traditionally raised poultry, not in wild or migratory birds (i.e., if HPAI H5N1 has been detected in wild or migratory birds but not in poultry in a country, that country would not be placed on the restricted list). Additionally, USDA has increased its monitoring of domestic commercial markets for illegally smuggled poultry and poultry products.

All imported live birds must be quarantined for 30 days at a USDA quarantine facility and tested for HPAI H5N1 before entering the country. Home quarantine and testing for AI also is required for returning U.S.-origin pet birds or performing or theatrical birds returning to the U.S.

The bans are enforced by:

- the CDC (see www.cdc.gov/flu/avian/outbreaks/embargo.htm),
- the Animal and Plant Health Inspection Service (APHIS) of the USDA (see www.aphis.usda.gov/vs/ncie/country.html#HPAI).
- The U.S. Fish and Wildlife Service under U.S. Customs and Border Protection of the Department of Homeland Security (see www.fws.gov/le/PubBulletins/PBImpRestrictionsBirdsH5N1 Update.htm).

Modifications to the Ban

- As of January 1, 2005 (69 FR 25820) and according to the Code of Federal Regulations (9 CFR 94.6), the ban was modified as follows:

"Carcasses, and parts or products of carcasses, of poultry, game birds, or other birds may be imported from a region where HPAI subtype H5N1 exists only if they are imported for scientific, educational or research purposes and the Administrator [of the Animal and Plant Health Inspection Service (APHIS) at the USDA] has determined that the importation can be made under conditions that will prevent the introduction of HPAI subtype H5N1 into the United States."

- On June 23, 2005, a technical amendment was published in the Federal Register (70 FR 36332) in which 9 CFR 94.6(e) was amended to specify that the carcasses specified are "unprocessed." This was added to remove the restriction on processed poultry products from the affected areas.

- The list of Countries/Areas Affected with Highly Pathogenic Avian Influenza subtype H5N1 and therefore included under 9 CFR 94.6 has grown considerably and is continuously updated. The current list is available at: http://www.aphis.usda.gov/vs/ncie/country.html#HPAI.

Illegal Importation of Birds – A Very Real Threat

Illegal importation of birds from H5N1-affected countries represents a major threat for the dissemination of H5N1 worldwide. Countries must be vigilant about this potential problem. For example, Belgium customs officials recently intercepted asymptomatic highly pathogenic avian influenza H5N1-infected crested hawk-eagles that were being smuggled from Thailand.[49] It is interesting to note that most of the live bird imports into the United States from the European Union in 2004 and 2005 were pet birds from Belgium.[50]

Legal Importation of Birds

It is of paramount importance that birds be quarantined for a significant period of time (e.g., the USDA has a 30-day quarantine period) when they are imported legally from other countries. For instance, 52 of 101 quarantined birds (Mesias) imported into the UK from Taiwan died (four were dead on arrival). Thirty-eight of the 52 dead birds were tested for H5N1. Tissues from these 38 birds were pooled into seven batches, five of which were positive for H5N1. It was concluded that, although the Mesias probably died from H5N1 infections, it may not have been the only cause. As a precaution, the remainder of the Mesias were euthanized. The H5N1 strain isolated from the Mesias most closely resembled a 2005 H5N1 isolate from Chinese ducks.[51]

Appendix H

History of Human Influenza Pandemics and Concern About a New Pandemic

Genetic studies indicate that aquatic birds, in particular, are the probable source of all influenza A virus strains found in other species.[22] The H5N1 virus is particularly worrisome because humans have no or little immunity to it. Luckily, not all novel influenza viruses are able to cause infection or pass freely from human-to-human. It is when they acquire this ability that they can cause a **pandemic**. If the infection cycle is restricted to bird-to-human transmission, there is little chance of a pandemic and the spread of the virus can be contained by eliminating infected birds and avoiding contact with infected birds.

Currently, only strains of three influenza A viral subtypes are considered **human flu viruses**. These refer to certain strains of **H1N1**, **H2N2**, and **H3N2** that can be efficiently transmitted between humans. There have been three well-documented pandemics caused by influenza A viruses. The Spanish flu, caused by an H1N1 virus, struck in 1918-1919 and killed 500,000 in the U.S. alone. In the second pandemic, the Asian flu caused by an H2N2 virus killed 70,000 in the U.S. and occurred in 1957-1958. In the most recent pandemic, the Hong Kong flu caused by an H3N2 virus killed 34,000 people in the U.S. and struck in 1968-1969. The second and third pandemics were the result of genetic reassortment whereby the circulating H1N1 virus acquired novel antigens H2 and N2 in 1957, and H3 in 1968, from avian sources. The typical annual U.S. flu epidemic (not pandemic) results in 200,000 hospitalizations and approximately 36,000 deaths with an overall mortality rate of 0.008% for those infected.[52] Since there has not been an influenza A pandemic for over 37 years, the feeling among experts is that we are long overdue. According to the Centers for Disease Control and Prevention (CDC):

> The severity of the next pandemic cannot be predicted, but modeling studies suggest that its effect in the United States

could be severe. In the absence of any control measures
(vaccination or drugs), it has been estimated that in the
United States a "medium–level" pandemic could cause
89,000 to 207,000 deaths, between 314,000 and 734,000
hospitalizations, 18 to 42 million outpatient visits, and
another 20 to 47 million people being sick. Between 15%
and 35% of the U.S. population could be affected by an
influenza pandemic, and the economic impact could
range between $71.3 and $166.5 billion.[52]

Increasing concern over the possibility of a pandemic has led
the World Health Organization (WHO) to develop a Global Influenza
Preparedness Plan.[53] The U.S. Department of Health and Human
Services (HHS) developed a National Strategy for Pandemic
Influenza (www.whitehouse.gov/homeland/nspi.pdf). The main
stages of a pandemic as defined by WHO have been summarized
below by CDC:[54]

Interpandemic Period

Novel influenza subtypes have not been detected in humans.

Phase 1: An influenza virus subtype that is known to have caused
human infection may be present in animals but the risk of human
infection or disease is considered to be low.

Phase 2: A circulating animal influenza virus subtype poses a
substantial risk of human disease.

The distinction between *phases 1* and *2* is based on the risk of
human infection or disease resulting from circulating strains in
animals. The distinction is based on various factors [e.g., pathogenicity in animals and humans, occurrence in domestic animals
and livestock or only in wildlife, whether the virus is enzootic
(occurs among animals in a certain area) or epizootic (epidemic
among animals), geographically localized or widespread, and/or
other scientific parameters] and their relative importance according
to current scientific knowledge.

www.osha.gov

Pandemic Alert Period

Phase 3: Human infection(s) with a novel subtype have occurred, but no human-to-human transmission, or at most only rare instances of spread to a close contact.

Phase 4: Small cluster(s) of human infections with limited human-to-human transmission but spread is highly localized, suggesting that the virus is not well adapted to humans.

Phase 5: Larger cluster(s) of human infections but human-to-human spread still localized, suggesting that the virus is becoming increasingly better adapted to humans, but may not yet be fully transmissible. At this point there is a **substantial pandemic risk**.

The distinction between *phases 3*, *4* and *5* is based on an assessment of the risk of a pandemic. Various factors [e.g., transmission rate, geographical location and spread, severity of illness, presence of genes from human strains (if derived from an animal strain), and/or other scientific parameters] and their relative importance according to current scientific knowledge may be considered.

Pandemic Period

Phase 6: **Pandemic**: increased and sustained person-to-person transmission in the general population.

According to the WHO plan, as of October 2006, the world is currently in phase 3, the first phase of the pandemic alert period.

Additional Sources of Information

There are other Federal agencies and international organizations that have additional resources on avian flu.

- Animal and Plant Health Inspection Service (APHIS) of the USDA provides online guidance on avian flu in birds and poultry products (www.aphis.usda.gov/hot_issues/avian_influenza/avian_influenza.shtml). Poultry employees and other farmworkers and pet shop employees should notify APHIS when they suspect birds may be infected with avian flu.

- Health and Human Services (HHS) has a website that is regularly updated and provides relevant information about avian influenza and information on pandemic preparedness and response (www.pandemicflu.gov).

- Centers for Disease Control and Prevention (CDC) has established avian flu public hotlines: Public: 800-CDC-INFO; TTY: 888-232-6348; and for Clinicians 877-554-4625. The CDC has additional online resources at: www.cdc.gov/flu/avian/index.htm.

- Center for Infectious Disease Research and Policy (CIDRAP), University of Minnesota provides continuously updated information on avian flu. (www.cidrap.umn.edu).

- The Environmental Protection Agency (EPA) has a website containing an avian influenza fact sheet and a list of registered disinfectant products for use in poultry and other agricultural and veterinary facilities at: www.epa.gov/pesticides/factsheets/avian_flu_products.htm.

- Food and Agriculture Organization of the United Nations (FAO). This website provides regular bulletins on avian flu. (http://www.fao.org/ag/againfo/home/en/home.html).

- ProMED-Mail – This website serves as a central site for news, updates, and discussions of outbreaks of emerging and re-emerging diseases that affect human health and provides up-to-date information on disease outbreaks around the world. (www.fas.org/promed/index.html).

- U.S. Fish and Wildlife Service, Division of Migratory Bird Management, Avian Influenza in Wild Birds—Sources of

Information. This website is very comprehensive and provides numerous links to Federal, state, and local websites concerning avian flu in wild birds. (www.fws.gov/migratorybirds/issues/AvianFlu/WBAvianFlu.htm# StateWildlifeAgencies).

- World Health Organization (WHO) has information on avian flu online. (www.who.int/csr/disease/avian_influenza/en).

- World Organization for Animal Health (OIE). This website has regular animal disease alerts. (www.oie.int/eng/en_index.htm).

- Physicians, employers and employees should contact their state or local health department (www.cdc.gov/mmwr/international/relres.html) to notify them of any symptomatic employees or suspected exposure incidents.

Numerous other sources of information about avian flu are available.[55]

For more information on safety and health resources, you may also want to consult the following:

- Directorate of Cooperative and State Programs (DCSP) home page at: www.osha.gov/dcsp/index.html. The site has links to the following:

State Plans

DCSP coordinates OSHA's activities with the OSHA-approved State occupational safety and health programs.

Outreach and Training

DSCP also provides or coordinates OSHA's outreach, compliance assistance, and training and education services, including:

- On-Site Consultation
- Compliance Assistance
- Small Business Assistance
- Training and Education

Appendix J

References

[1] Centers for Disease Control and Prevention, Interim Guidance for Protection of Persons Involved in U.S. Avian Influenza Outbreak Disease Control and Eradication Activities. (www.cdc.gov/flu/avian/professional/protect-guid.htm).

[2] Centers for Disease Control and Prevention, *Updated Interim Guidance for Laboratory Testing of Persons with Suspected Infection with Avian Influenza A (H5N1) Virus in the United States, June 7, 2006.* (www.phppo.cdc.gov/HAN/ArchiveSys/ViewMsgV.asp?AlertNum=00246).

[3] Centers for Disease Control and Prevention, Interim Recommendations for Infection Control in Healthcare Facilities Caring for Patients with Known or Suspected Avian Influenza. (www.cdc.gov/flu/avian/professional/infect-control.htm).

[4] Simeonsson, K. et al. 2004. Influenza vaccination of healthcare workers: institutional strategies for improving rates. N.C. Med. J. 65:323-329.

[5] Lu, X. et al. 2003. Pathogenicity and antigenicity of a new influenza A (H5N1) virus isolated from duck meat. J. Med. Virol. 69:553-559.

[6] Mase, M.E. et al. 2005. Isolation of a genotypically unique H5N1 influenza virus from duck meat imported into Japan from China. Virology, 339:101-109.

[7] Centers for Disease Control and Prevention, Update: Guidelines and Recommendations Interim Guidance about Avian Influenza A (H5N1) for U.S. Citizens Living Abroad. (www.cdc.gov/travel/other/avian_flu_ig_americans_abroad_032405.htm).

[8] Centers for Disease Control and Prevention, Interim Guidance for Airline Flight Crews and Persons Meeting Passengers Arriving from Areas with Avian Influenza. (www.cdc.gov/travel/other/avian_flu_ig_airlines_021804.htm).

[9] Centers for Disease Control and Prevention, Outbreak Notice - Update: Human Infection with Avian Influenza A (H5N1) Virus in Asia. (www.cdc.gov/travel/other/avian_influenza_se_asia_2005.htm).

[10] Infectious Diseases Society of America (IDSA), Avian Influenza (Bird Flu): Agricultural and Wildlife Considerations. Last updated May 12, 2006. (www.cidrap.umn.edu/cidrap/content/influenza/avianflu/biofacts/avflu.html).

[11] World Health Organization, Avian influenza – fact sheet. 15 January, 2004. (http://www.who.int/csr/don/2004_01_15/en).

[12] Enserink, M. 2005. Veterinary scientists shore up defenses against bird flu. Science 308:341.

[13] Avian Influenza Technical Task Force, FAO – Rome & Bangkok. 2005. Update on the avian influenza situation (as of 12/11/2005) – Issue no. 36. FAOAIDEnews. Avian Influenza Disease Emergency. (www.fao.org/ag/againfo/subjects/documents/ai/AVIbull036.pdf).

[14] World Health Organization, Avian influenza - Avian influenza ("bird flu") and the significance of its transmission to humans. 15 January, 2004. (http://www.who.int/mediacentre/factsheets/avian_influenza/en/print.html).

[15] World Health Organization, Cumulative number of confirmed human cases of avian influenza A/(H5N1) reported to WHO. 29 May 2006. (www.who.int/csr/disease/avian_influenza/country/cases_table_2006_05_29/en/index.html).

[16] Bridges, C.B., et al. 2002. Risk of influenza A (H5N1) infection among poultry workers, Hong Kong, 1997-1998. J. Infect. Dis. 185:1005-10.

[17] Liem, N.T. and W. Lim. 2005. Lack of H5N1 avian influenza transmission to hospital employees, Hanoi, 2004. Emer. Infect. Dis. 11:210-215.

[18] Choi, Y.K., et al. 2005. Influenza virus infection of pigs by using viruses isolated in Vietnam and Thailand in 2004. J. Virol. 79:10821-10825.

[19] Shortridge, K.F., et al. 1998. Characterization of avian H5N1 influenza viruses from poultry in Hong Kong. Virology 252:331-342.

[20] Kuiken, T., et al. 2005. Avian H5N1 influenza in cats. Science 306:241.

[21] Avian Influenza Technical Task Force, FAO – Rome & Bangkok. 2005. Update on the avian influenza situation (as of 31/07/2005) – Issue no. 32. FAOAIDEnews. Avian Influenza Disease Emergency.

(www.fao.org/ag/againfo/subjects/documents/ai/AVIbull032.pdf).

[22] Reed, K.D., et al. 2003. Birds, migration and emerging zoonoses: West Nile virus, Lyme disease, influenza A and enteropathogens. Clin. Med. Res. 1:5-12.

[23] Liu, J., et al. 2005. Highly pathogenic H5N1 influenza virus infection in migratory birds. Science, 309:1206.

[24] State of Alaska Epidemiology Bulletin No. 21, Sept. 1, 2005. H5N1 Avian Influenza: What Alaskans Need to Know. (http://www.epi.alaska.gov/bulletins/docs/b2005_21.pdf).

[25] USGS National Wildlife Health Center. USDA, DOI and HHS expand screening for highly pathogenic H5N1 avian influenza in migratory birds. USDA, DOI and HHS Spotlight Interagency Readiness Plans. March 20, 2006. (www.nwhc.usgs.gov/disease_information/avian_influenza/department_of_the_interior_H5N1_brief.jsp).

[26] Osterholm, M.T. 2005. Preparing for the next pandemic. N. Engl. J. Med. 352:1839-1842.

[27] Cox, N.J. and K. Subbarao. 2000. Global epidemiology of influenza: Past and present. Ann. Rev. Med. 51:407-421.

[28] Crawford, P.C., et al. 2005. Transmission of equine influenza to dogs. Science 310:482-485.

[29] Suzuki, Y. 2005. Sialobiology of influenza – molecular mechanism of host range variation in influenza viruses. Biol. Pharm. Bull. 28:399-408.

[30] Normille, D. 2005. Are wild birds to blame? Science 310:426-428.

[31] Chin, P.S., et al. 2002. Molecular evolution on H6 influenza viruses from poultry in southeastern China: Prevalence of H6N1 influenza viruses possessing seven A/Hong Kong/156/97 (H5N1)-like genes in poultry. J. Virol. 76:507-516.

[32] Centers for Disease Control and Prevention, Avian Influenza Infection in Humans. (www.cdc.gov/flu/avian/gen-info/avian-flu-humans.htm).

[33] Li, K.S., et al. 2004. Genesis of a highly pathogenic and potentially pandemic H5N1 influenza virus in eastern Asia. Nature 430:209-213.

[34] Guan, Y., et al. 2004. H5N1 influenza: A protean pandemic threat. Proc Natl Acad Sci USA. 101:8156-8161.

[35] Lee, C.W., et al. 2005. Characterization of highly pathogenic H5N1 avian influenza A viruses isolated from South Korea. J. Virol. 79:3692-3702.

[36] Mase, M., et al. 2005. Characterization of H5N1 influenza A viruses isolated during the 2003-2004 influenza outbreaks in Japan. Virology 332:167-176.

[37] World Health Organization, Laboratory study of H5N1 viruses in domestic ducks: main findings, 29 October 2004. (www.who.int/csr/disease/avian_influenza/labstudy_2004_10_29/en/print.html).

[38] U.S. Geological Survey National Wildlife Health Center. Wildlife Health Bulletin #05-02. (www.nwhc.usgs.gov/research/WHB/WHB_05_02.html).

[39] DeMarco, MA, et al. 2003. Long-term monitoring for avian influenza viruses in wild bird species in Italy. Vet. Res. Comm. 27 Suppl. 1: 107-114.

[40] Smith, GJD, et al., 2006. Evolution and adaptation of H5N1 influenza virus in avian and human hosts in Indonesia and Vietnam. Virology. In Press.

[41] Stallknecht, DE, et al., 1990. Persistence of avian influenza viruses in water. Avian Dis. 34:406-411.

[42] Lu, et al. 2003. Survival of avian influenza virus H7N2 in SPF chickens and their environments. Avian Dis. 47:1015-21.

[43] Stallknecht, DE, et al. 1990. Effects of pH, temperature, and salinity on persistence of avian influenza viruses in water. Avian Dis. 34:412-418.

[44] 2005 OIE Terrestrial Animal Health Code. Appendix 3.8.9. Guidelines for the surveillance of avian influenza. Article 3.8.9.1.

[45] Beigel, J.H., et al. 2005. Current concepts: Avian influenza A (H5N1) infection in humans. N. Engl. J. Med. 353:1374-1385.

[46] Apisarnthanarak, A., et al. 2004. Atypical avian influenza (H5N1). Emerg. Infect. Dis. 10:1321-1324.

[47] de Jong, M.D., et al. 2005. Fatal avian influenza A (H5N1) in a child presenting with diarrhea followed by coma. N. Engl. J. Med. 352:686-691.

[48] Centers for Disease Control and Prevention, Embargo of Birds from Specified Southeast Asian Countries, General Information. (www.cdc.gov/flu/avian/outbreaks/embargo.htm).

[49] Van Borm, S., et al. 2005. Highly pathogenic H5N1 influenza virus in smuggled Thai eagles, Belgium. Emerg. Infect. Dis. 11:702-705.

[50] USDA Veterinary Services, Highly Pathogenic Avian Influenza, Outbreak Summary for European Union, March 6, 2006, Impact Worksheet. Available at: http://www.aphis.usda.gov/ vs/ceah/cei/taf/iw_2006_files/foreign/hpaieusum041906_files/hpaie usum041906.htm).

[51] National Emergency Epidemiology Group. 11 November 2005. Epidemiology report on avian influenza in quarantine premises in Essex. 9 pp. (http://www.defra.gov.uk/animalh/diseases/notifiable/disease/ai/pd f/ai-epidemrep111105.pdf)

[52] Centers for Disease Control and Prevention, Key Facts About Pandemic Influenza. (www.cdc.gov/flu/pandemic/keyfacts.htm).

[53] World Health Organization, Global Influenza Preparedness Plan. The Role of WHO and Recommendations for National Measures before and during Pandemics. (www.who.int/csr/ resources/publications/influenza/WHO_CDS_CSR_GIP_2005_5.pdf).

[54] Centers for Disease Control and Prevention, Stages of a Pandemic. (www.cdc.gov/flu/pandemic/phases.htm).

[55] Larkin, M. 2006. Keeping abreast of avian influenza developments. Lancet Infect. Dis. 6:269-270.

OSHA Assistance

OSHA can provide extensive help through a variety of programs, including technical assistance about effective safety and health programs, state plans, workplace consultations, voluntary protection programs, strategic partnerships, training and education, and more. An overall commitment to workplace safety and health can add value to your business, to your workplace and to your life.

Safety and Health Program Management Guidelines

Effective management of employee safety and health protection is a decisive factor in reducing the extent and severity of work-related injuries and illnesses and their related costs. In fact, an effective safety and health program forms the basis of good employee protection and can save time and money (about $4 for every dollar spent) and increase productivity and reduce employee injuries, illnesses and related workers' compensation costs.

To assist employers and employees in developing effective safety and health programs, OSHA published recommended *Safety and Health Program Management Guidelines* (54 *Federal Register* (16): 3904-3916, January 26, 1989). These voluntary guidelines apply to all places of employment covered by OSHA.

The guidelines identify four general elements critical to the development of a successful safety and health management program:

- Management leadership and employee involvement.
- Work analysis.
- Hazard prevention and control.
- Safety and health training.

The guidelines recommend specific actions, under each of these general elements, to achieve an effective safety and health program. The *Federal Register* notice is available online at www.osha.gov

State Programs

The Occupational Safety and Health Act of 1970 (OSH Act) encourages states to develop and operate their own job safety and

health plans. OSHA approves and monitors these plans. Twenty-four states, Puerto Rico and the Virgin Islands currently operate approved state plans: 22 cover both private and public (state and local government) employment; Connecticut, New Jersey, New York and the Virgin Islands cover the public sector only. States and territories with their own OSHA-approved occupational safety and health plans must adopt standards identical to, or at least as effective as, the Federal standards.

Consultation Services

Consultation assistance is available on request to employers who want help in establishing and maintaining a safe and healthful workplace. Largely funded by OSHA, the service is provided at no cost to the employer. Primarily developed for smaller employers with more hazardous operations, the consultation service is delivered by state governments employing professional safety and health consultants. Comprehensive assistance includes an appraisal of all mechanical systems, work practices and occupational safety and health hazards of the workplace and all aspects of the employer's present job safety and health program. In addition, the service offers assistance to employers in developing and implementing an effective safety and health program. No penalties are proposed or citations issued for hazards identified by the consultant. OSHA provides consultation assistance to the employer with the assurance that his or her name and firm and any information about the workplace will not be routinely reported to OSHA enforcement staff.

Under the consultation program, certain exemplary employers may request participation in OSHA's Safety and Health Achievement Recognition Program (SHARP). Eligibility for participation in SHARP includes receiving a comprehensive consultation visit, demonstrating exemplary achievements in workplace safety and health by abating all identified hazards and developing an excellent safety and health program.

Employers accepted into SHARP may receive an exemption from programmed inspections (not complaint or accident investigation inspections) for a period of one year. For more information concerning consultation assistance, see the OSHA website at www.osha.gov

Voluntary Protection Programs (VPP)

Voluntary Protection Programs and on-site consultation services, when coupled with an effective enforcement program, expand employee protection to help meet the goals of the OSH Act. The three levels of VPP are Star, Merit, and Star Demonstration designed to recognize outstanding achievements by companies that have successfully incorporated comprehensive safety and health programs into their total management system. The VPPs motivate others to achieve excellent safety and health results in the same outstanding way as they establish a cooperative relationship between employers, employees and OSHA.

For additional information on VPP and how to apply, contact the OSHA regional offices listed at the end of this publication.

Strategic Partnership Program

OSHA's Strategic Partnership Program, the newest member of OSHA's cooperative programs, helps encourage, assist and recognize the efforts of partners to eliminate serious workplace hazards and achieve a high level of employee safety and health. Whereas OSHA's Consultation Program and VPP entail one-on-one relationships between OSHA and individual worksites, most strategic partnerships seek to have a broader impact by building cooperative relationships with groups of employers and em-ployees. These partnerships are voluntary, cooperative relation-ships between OSHA, employers, employee representatives and others (e.g., trade unions, trade and professional associations, universities and other government agencies).

For more information on this and other cooperative programs, contact your nearest OSHA office, or visit OSHA's website at www.osha.gov

Alliance Programs

The Alliance Program enables organizations committed to workplace safety and health to collaborate with OSHA to prevent injuries and illnesses in the workplace. OSHA and the Alliance participants work together to reach out to, educate and lead the nation's employers and their employees in improving and advanc-ing workplace safety and health.

Groups that can form an Alliance with OSHA include employers, labor unions, trade or professional groups, educational institutions and government agencies. In some cases, organizations may be building on existing relationships with OSHA that were developed through other cooperative programs.

There are few formal program requirements for Alliances and the agreements do not include an enforcement component. However, OSHA and the participating organizations must define, implement and meet a set of short- and long-term goals that fall into three categories: training and education; outreach and communication; and promoting the national dialogue on workplace safety and health.

OSHA Training and Education

OSHA area offices offer a variety of information services, such as compliance assistance, technical advice, publications, audiovisual aids and speakers for special engagements. OSHA's Training Institute in Arlington Heights, IL, provides basic and advanced courses in safety and health for Federal and state compliance officers, state consultants, Federal agency personnel, and private sector employers, employees and their representatives.

The OSHA Training Institute also has established OSHA Training Institute Education Centers to address the increased demand for its courses from the private sector and from other Federal agencies. These centers are nonprofit colleges, universities and other organizations that have been selected after a competition for participation in the program.

OSHA also provides funds to nonprofit organizations, through grants, to conduct workplace training and education in subjects where OSHA believes there is a lack of workplace training. Grants are awarded annually. Grant recipients are expected to contribute 20 percent of the total grant cost.

For more information on grants, training and education, contact the OSHA Training Institute, Office of Training and Education, 2020 South Arlington Heights Road, Arlington Heights, IL 60005, (847) 297-4810 or see "Outreach" on OSHA's website at www.osha.gov. For further information on any OSHA program, contact your nearest OSHA area or regional office listed at the end of this publication.

Information Available Electronically

OSHA has a variety of materials and tools available on its website at www.osha.gov. These include *e-Tools* such as *Expert Advisors, Electronic Compliance Assistance Tools (e-cats), Technical Links*; regulations, directives and publications; videos and other information for employers and employees. OSHA's software programs and compliance assistance tools walk you through challenging safety and health issues and common problems to find the best solutions for your workplace.

A wide variety of OSHA materials, including standards, interpretations, directives, and more, can be purchased on CD-ROM from the U.S. Government Printing Office, Superintendent of Documents, phone toll-free (866) 512-1800.

OSHA Publications

OSHA has an extensive publications program. For a listing of free or sales items, visit OSHA's website at www.osha.gov or contact the OSHA Publications Office, U.S. Department of Labor, 200 Constitution Avenue, NW, N-3101, Washington, DC 20210. Telephone (202) 693-1888 or fax to (202) 693-2498.

Contacting OSHA

To report an emergency, file a complaint or seek OSHA advice, assistance or products, call (800) 321-OSHA or contact your nearest OSHA regional or area office listed at the end of this publication. The teletypewriter (TTY) number is (877) 889-5627.

You can also file a complaint online and obtain more information on OSHA Federal and state programs by visiting OSHA's website at www.osha.gov

OSHA Regional Offices

Region I
(CT,* ME, MA, NH, RI, VT*)
JFK Federal Building, Room E340
Boston, MA 02203
(617) 565-9860

Region II
(NJ,* NY,* PR,* VI*)
201 Varick Street, Room 670
New York, NY 10014
(212) 337-2378

Region III
(DE, DC, MD,* PA, VA,* WV)
The Curtis Center
170 S. Independence Mall West
Suite 740 West
Philadelphia, PA 19106-3309
(215) 861-4900

Region IV
(AL, FL, GA, KY,* MS, NC,* SC,* TN*)
61 Forsyth Street, SW
Atlanta, GA 30303
(404) 562-2300

Region V
(IL, IN,* MI,* MN,* OH, WI)
230 South Dearborn Street
Room 3244
Chicago, IL 60604
(312) 353-2220

Region VI
(AR, LA, NM,* OK, TX)
525 Griffin Street, Room 602
Dallas, TX 75202
(214) 767-4731 or 4736 x224

Region VII
(IA,* KS, MO, NE)
City Center Square
1100 Main Street, Suite 800
Kansas City, MO 64105
(816) 426-5861

Region VIII
(CO, MT, ND, SD, UT,* WY*)
1999 Broadway, Suite 1690
PO Box 46550
Denver, CO 80202-5716
(720) 264-6550

Region IX
(American Samoa, AZ,* CA,* HI,* NV,*
Northern Mariana Islands)
71 Stevenson Street, Room 420
San Francisco, CA 94105
(415) 975-4310

Region X
(AK,* ID, OR,* WA*)
1111 Third Avenue, Suite 715
Seattle, WA 98101-3212
(206) 553-5930

* These states and territories operate their own OSHA-approved job safety and health programs (Connecticut, New Jersey, New York and the Virgin Islands plans cover public employees only). States with approved programs must adopt standards identical to, or at least as effective as, the Federal standards.

Note: To get contact information for OSHA Area Offices, OSHA-approved State Plans and OSHA Consultation Projects, please visit us online at www.osha.gov or call us at 1-800-321-OSHA.

www.ingramcontent.com/pod-product-compliance
Lightning Source LLC
Chambersburg PA
CBHW051817170526
45167CB00005B/2045